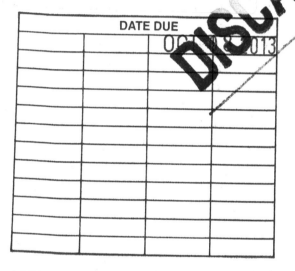

USA Citizenship Interview and Test Practice Made Easy

Published by Lakewood Publishing
1710 Moorpark Rd., Suite #213
Thousand Oaks, CA 91360

ISBN: 978-1-936583-25-6 (paperback)

Library of Congress Control Number: 2011941410

1. Citizenship, United States, America, U.S. 2. naturalization, citizenship
3 citizenship test, new test 4. United States – USCIS new test October 2008
5.. United States – civics, government, history 6.. immigration
7. 4 English – language
I. Citizenship, American   II. Title

USA Citizenship Interview and Test Practice Made Easy

J.S. Aaron

Also Available from Lakewood Publishing

Guide for New Immigrants: **Welcome to the United States**
ISBN: 978-1-936583-42-3 (paperback)
ISBN: 978-1-936583-18-8 (ebook)

Guía para Inmigrantes Nuevos: **Bienvenidos a los Estados Unidos de América**
ISBN: 978-1-936583-43-0 (paperback)
ISBN: 978-1-936583-37-9 (ebook)

*Learn About the United States: Quick Civics Lessons for the New NaturalizationTest
ISBN: 978-1-936583-01-0 (hardback)
ISBN: 978-0-9793538-1-9 (paperback)
ISBN 978-0-9793538-9-5 (digital/ebook)

U.S. Citizenship Test Questions in 5 Languages--English, Spanish, Chinese, Tagalog and Vietnamese
English -Español - 中英 - Tagalog - tiếng Việt
ISBN: 978-1-936583-11-9 (hardback)
ISBN: 978-1-936583-10-2 (paperback)

*U.S. Citizenship Test (English edition): 100 Questions and Answers Includes a Flash Card Format for Easy Practice
ISBN: 978-1-936583-04-1

*U.S.Citizenship Test (English and Spanish - Español y Inglés) **100 Bilingual Questions and Answers** 100 Preguntas y respuestas del exámen de la ciudadanía (2011-2012)
ISBN: 978-1-936583-07-2

US Citizenship Test (Chinese-English 中英) 100 Bilingual Questions and Answers 新版公民入籍歸化考試的 100 道考題與答案
ISBN: 978-1-936583-05-8

U.S. Citizenship Test: 100 Bilingual Questions and Answers (Filipino – Tagalog – Ingles – English) **100 Katanungan at Sagot para sa Iksamen sa U.S. Naturalisasyon**
ISBN: : 978-1-936583-09-6

U.S. Citizenship Test: (Vietnamese - English - tiếng Việt - tiếng Anh) **100 câu hỏi và câu trả lời để chuẩn bị cho kỳ thi quốc tich Mỹ**
ISBN: 978-0-936583-12-6

Learn How You Can:

Get a Green Card

Apply for "Deferred Action for Childhood Arrival"

Prepare for Your Interview

Pass the U.S. Citizenship Test

Become a USA Citizen

Flashcards

Digital flashcards—fully linked—are available for this book at ebook stores as:

100 Flashcard Questions and Answers for U.S. Citizenship Test Practice ISBN: 9781936583249

Contact us:

Lakewood Publishing, 1710 N. Moorpark Road, Suite 213, Thousand Oaks, CA. 91360

www.lakewoodpublishing.com

You can follow J.S. Aaron on Twitter: @JS_Aaron
And on Facebook: J.s. Aaron or Welcome ESL
www.welcomeesl.com

"I lift my lamp beside the golden door."

-from the poem, "The New Colossus",
inscribed on the base of the Statue of Liberty
Emma Lazarus (1883)

Contents

Section 1: Becoming a Citizen

Different Words Can Mean the Same Thing   4

1 Introduction   5

2 How to Become a U.S. Citizen   17

3 How to Get a Permanent Resident Visa   27

4 Applying for Citizenship   47

5 The Citizenship Test: "What Do I Need To Know?"   69

6 Special Circumstances and Exemptions   79

Section 2: Where to Go for Information and Help

7 Websites and Other Helpful Resources   89

Section 3: Citizenship Test Practice

8 "What Happens At My Citizenship Interview?"   97

9 Speaking English: Know Your N-400 Form   107

10 Reading Test Practice   147

11 Writing Test Practice   155

12 Vocabulary for Reading and Writing: 165
The 500 Most Frequently Used English Words

13 Practice Sentences for Reading and Writing   213

14 Civics Practice: Question and Answers   225

15 Civics Practice: Multiple Choice   251

16 Civics Practice: Questions Only   277

17 65/20: Civics Questions if you are 65+ years   287

18 100 Civics Flashcards   301

Appendix: "Deferred Action for Childhood Arrivals"   373
How to qualify, How to apply, USCIS Questions & Answers
for visa program for undocumented immigrants brought to
the U.S. as children.

Index   393

How to Become a U.S. Citizen

1

Introduction

Different Words That Can Mean the Same Thing

In the citizenship process, some words and phrases are used that mean the same thing. Here is a list of some common words.

Naturalization and Citizenship

"Citizenship" and "Naturalization" can both describe the process of becoming a U.S. citizen. The U.S. government usually calls this process "naturalization" but most people call it "applying for citizenship" or "becoming a U.S. citizen".

Citizenship Interview - Citizenship Test - Naturalization

These all describe the time when a US government representative (USCIS officer) interviews you to see if you can become a U.S. citizen.

USCIS – INS

The part of the government responsible for immigration used to be called the INS (Immigration and Naturalization Service). Now it is called USCIS (U.S. Citizenship and Immigration Service). It is part of the Department of Homeland Security.

USCIS officer – Interviewer

The person who will interview you and decide if you are ready to become a citizen is called a representative, or "officer", of the U.S. government. He is not a policeman or a military officer.

Permanent Resident – PR – green card

Your permanent resident visa (P.R.) is also called your green card. When you have this card, it means that you can legally live in the United States as long as you want.

1
Introduction

Do You Want to Become a U.S. Citizen?

United States citizenship can give you many new opportunities. There are educational, work and lifestyle benefits of being a U.S. citizen. American citizens have the protection of U.S. laws, and they can usually travel abroad without any visa problems.

As a U.S. citizen, or as a permanent resident, you can also help your immediate family members become citizens. Your U.S. citizenship can help your spouse, parents and children find new educational or career opportunities in the United States. But giving up citizenship in your native country is often not an easy decision. For many people who become U.S. citizens, it can be a long time until they see their native country, relatives and friends again.

Many immigrants also do not know English when they arrive in the U.S.. Even if they are busy with a job and a family, they need to find time to learn a new language—and English is one of the most difficult languages in the world, especially if you are learning it as an adult.

Also, in times of international conflicts, immigrants may feel loyalty to the U.S. and also to the country where they were born. But when you become a U.S. citizen, you promise to be loyal only to the United States. All of these things make becoming a U.S. citizen one of the most important decisions that you can make.

Permanent Resident Visa

There are many kinds of visas that allow you to live or work in the United States temporarily. But the permanent resident visa allows you to live legally in the U.S. for as long as you want.

Rights of a Permanent Resident

Immigrants with permanent resident visas have many of the same rights as U.S. citizens. As a permanent resident, you have the right to:

- Live and work permanently in the U.S.;
- Apply for U.S. citizenship;
- Have the protection of U.S. laws;
- Apply for visas for your husband or wife and unmarried children;
- Apply for Social Security, Supplemental Security Income (SSI), and Medicare benefits;
- Own property in the United States;
- Apply for a driver's license;
- Leave and return to the U.S. easily;
- Get public education and go to college;
- Join the U.S. military.

Responsibilities of a Permanent Resident

Permanent residents also have responsibilites. As a permanent resident you must:

- Obey the laws of the United States;
- Report your income and pay your taxes;
- Support the Constitution of the United States;
- Men age 18 through 25 must register with the Selective Service (U.S. military);
- Keep your immigration status current;
- Carry your Permanent Resident visa;
- Tell the Department of Homeland Security within 10 days of moving to a new address.

It is easy to live in the U.S. as a permanent resident. Permanent residents can legally live in the United States forever and still keep citizenship in their native country.

But even though it is easy to live in the U.S. as a permanent resident, every year more than 100,000 immigrants give up their permanent resident visas because they want to become American citizens.

Immigrants who become U.S. citizens have studied hard to learn about the history and culture of the United States. Often, they have also spent many years learning English. As anyone who has ever attended a citizenship ceremony knows, there is a wonderful feeling of excitement and pride in the room on that special day. These new U.S. citizens have worked hard to accomplish their goals, and they have made a commitment to their new country. They are proud to be Americans.

How to Become a U.S. Citizen

It can take many years to become a U.S. citizen, but it is not a difficult process if you know the steps. This book will help you understand what you need to do and what you need to know to succeed.

You will learn....

- the 10 Steps to Citizenship
- who qualifies for a permanent resident visa
- how to answer questions for the interview
- how to practice for the civics and English tests
- what civics to know if you are 65+ years old
- the USCIS reading and writing vocabulary
- who qualifies for special exemptions
- websites, video links and helpful addresses
- 100 flashcards for civics practice

This book has four sections. Each section tells you important information about how to become a U.S. citizen.

Section 1: The Steps to Citizenship

In this section, chapters 1 - 6 describe how to become a U.S. citizen. Here, you will quickly find the most important information to know when you are preparing for citizenship.

Chapter 1 is an introduction to citizenship.

Chapter 2 shows you the most important steps to take to become a citizen.

Chapter 3 lists the most common ways to get a permanent resident visa, the first step in the citizenship process.

Chapter 4 explains how to become a citizen after you have your permanent resident visa. Use this chapter to keep a record of your progress.

Chapter 5 tells what the citizenship test is and how to pass it.

Chapter 6 explains how to qualify for exemptions, exceptions and modifications to the citizenship test.

Section 2: Helpful Websites, Addresses and Phone Numbers

Chapter 7 lists many useful websites, addresses, phone numbers and email addresses where you can get help and information.

Section 3: Practice for Your Citizenship Tests and Interview

Chapters 8-17 give you practice for your citizenship interview and English tests.

Many people do not know what to expect at their citizenship interview. The activities in Section 3 let you practice the skills that you will need to become a U.S. citizen. In Section 3, you will learn how to prepare for all four parts of the USCIS test.

Chapter 8   describes the citizenship interview and tests and tells you what the passing scores are.

Chapter 9   gives you practice with the citizenship interview.

Chapter 10   has practice for the USCIS reading test.

Chapter 11   helps you prepare for the USCIS writing test.

Chapter 12   lists useful English vocabulary and has space for you to practice reading and writing these words.

Chapter 13   gives you sentences to read and write in English.

Chapter 14 – 17 have many different ways to learn the civics questions.

Section 4: Flashcards for Civics Practice

Chapter 18 gives you all of the 100 civics questions and answers in a flashcard format for easier practice.

You can take these pages out of this book and cut them into separate "cards" for each question. This way, it is easy to see how many answers you know and how many answers you need to learn.

More Resources at the "Welcome ESL" Website
www.welcomeesl.com

Our *Welcome ESL* website has many free study materials. These include links to websites where you can practice with self-correcting civics questions and listen to radio broadcasts for English language learners. You can also try spelling, vocabulary, and writing activities and even some interactive games to practice reading and writing in English.

Links to USCIS

The USCIS website has excellent, up-to-date information. But it is often difficult to find forms and answers to questions at the USCIS website. If you have a problem at the USCIS website, go to *Welcome ESL* (www.welcomeesl.com) and use our easy links to USCIS information. For example, the www.welcomeesl.com website has links to the USCIS N-400 citizenship form..

At *Welcome ESL*, you will also find a link where you can practice a multiple choice USCIS civics test that will be automatically corrected for you online. There are also links to videos from USCIS that explain how to become a U.S. citizen. These are in Spanish and in English.

Finally, at www.welcomeesl.com you can see a video of a recent citizenship ceremony at the White House. And you can watch USCIS citizenship interviews in Spanish and English.

Recommended Bilingual Books in Chinese, Tagalog, Vietnamese and Spanish

USCIS has translated all 100 civics questions and answers from English into Spanish, Chinese, Vietnamese and Tagalog. To review these questions in a way that is easy to study, we recommend our bilingual test preparation series, *U.S. Citizenship Test Questions*. This six-book series includes an English-only book (with flashcards) and a unique mulitilingual book that has all of the 100 civics test questions and answers in the five translations that USCIS has made available. Each book in the series includes the English translation and all of the recommended USCIS vocabulary.

Reading questions in your native language can be a very helpful way to understand difficult new vocabulary and ideas iin English. Bilingual study guides like these can be helpful in a classroom or when you are studying alone.

Bilingual Study Guides for People Over 65 Years Old

People over 65 years old who have been permanent residents for over 20 years can take the civics test in their native language. Bilingual books are very useful for people who will be tested this way. After reading test questions in English and their native language, many permanent residents feel more confident. Many decide to take the civics test in English instead of their native language.

Other Recommended Study Aids

At Lakewood Publishing our goal is to make citizenship materials that are affordable and easy to use. For this reason, we have citizenship books in many formats—as paperback and hardback books, ebooks and as digital flashcards. If you have an e-reader, you can also practice the civics questions and answers with our fully linked digtal flashcards, *100 Flashcards for U.S. Citizenship Test Practice*.

We also have two guides to living in the United States: *Guide for New Immigrants*, and, in Spanish, *Guía para Inmigrantes Nuevos*. Also *Learn About the United States: Quick Civics Lessons for the Naturalization Test* is available as a paperback, hardback or ebook. It has all of the civics questions, but includes longer readings that explain the cultural and historic importance of each civics answer.

At Lakewood Publishing, we hope that preparing for U.S. citizenship will create new opportunities or you—and that you will enjoy a wonderful future as an American citizen.

Deferred Action for Childhood Arrivals. This section has basic questions and answer on this new program. For more detailed explanations, see the Appendix, pp. 373-391.

Deferred Action for Childhood Arrivals

**President Obama's New Visa Program of June 15, 2012
For more information, see Appendix, pp. 373-391**

On June 15, 2012, President Obama, through executive order, changed one part of the law that affects undocumented immigrants living in the United States. On August 15, 2012, this new program, "Deferred Action for Childhood Arrivals" began. It allows qualified young immigrants to stay in the U.S. legally, without fear of deportation. They can apply to stay in the U.S. for 2 years, and then can apply for an extension.

"Deferred Action for Childhood Arrivals" will permit many young immigrants to legally go to school, get a driver's license, and work in the United States without fear of deportation.

Questions and Answers

Question: Who qualifies for this program?

Answer: Undocumented immigrants who

*were brought to the United States when they were under 16 years old,

*have lived in the U.S. for at least 5 years,

*are now under 30 years old, and

*have committed no felonies or other serious crimes.

And

*They must also be an honorably discharged veteran of the Coast Guard or armed forces, or a high school graduate, or have received a GED (high school graduation equivalency certificate).

Not eligible. Immigrants will not be eligible for the program if they "pose a threat to national security or public safety," including having been convicted of a felony or a significant misdemeanor.

Question: How many people will be affected?

Answer: An estimated 800,000 people are expected to request deferred action on deportation.

Question: Isn't this a good reason for more people to come illegally to the United States?

Answer: No. President Obama's order only applies to people who are already living in the United States and who were at least 5 years old—and under 16—when they were brought here.

Question: Why was the change made?

Answer: Janet Napolitano, the head of the Department of Homeland Security, said that the Obama administration wanted to concentrate its resources on deporting Ilegal immigrants who had committed crimes.

Napolitano said, "This grant of deferred action is not immunity. It is not amnesty. It is an exercise of discretion so that these young people are not in the removal system. It will help us to continue to streamline immigration enforcement and ensure that resources are not spent pursuing the removal of low-priority cases involving productive young people."

Question: What will happen to people who are already being deported?

Answer: Immigration and Customs Enforcement, as well as Customs and Border Protection, were told to immediately begin reviewing each current deportation case and to stop the deportation of immigrants who qualify for this program.

Question: Will these undocumented immigrants be able to vote in U.S. elections?

Answer: No. Only U.S. citizens can vote.

Question: Will this protection from deportation last forever?

Answer: No. It will stop proceedings against qualified immigrants for two years. After that, they will need to apply for renewal.

Question: Will all illegal immigrants get work permits now?

Answer: No. Undocumented immigrants who qualify for the program will be given work permits on a case-by-case basis.

Question: Will I need to pay to make this change?

Answer: On the day this was announced, an Obama administration official told reporters that most immigrants will probably need to go to USCIS to pay a fee and provide certain documents (for example, proof of high school graduation or military service.) You should check with the USCIS website for any updates on fees.

Question: Can opponents have this order overturned?

Answer: Several members of Congress have publicly opposed the new order. Some, like U.S. Congressman Steve King (Republican-Iowa), say they will sue to block the president's policy and then have the courts overturn it. It is unlikely that this will be successful. More likely, Congress will eventually pass a new law that will add to, not take away from, President Obama's decision.

Question: Is this the same as the Dream Act?

Answer: No. The Dream Act that was defeated in Congress in 2010, wanted to give qualified young immigrants green cards and a way to become citizens.

Question: Will these undocumented immigrants now be able to become citizens?

Answer: No. Only Congress can pass a law to change the citizenship requirements.

For more information, see Appendix, pp. 373-391

2

How to Become a U.S. Citizen

2

How to Become a U.S. Citizen

U.S. citizenship begins with getting a Permanent Resident visa. In most cases, you cannot become a United States citizen without one.

The checklist below shows you the most important steps to citizenhip. It begins with becoming a Permanent Resident. You will see a more detailed citizenship checklist in Chapter 4, but the list below is a good place to begin. Check (√) anything that you have already done.

Checklist: 10 Steps to Citizenship √

__Step 1: Become a Permanent Resident

You must become a Permanent Resident before you can become a U.S. citizen. It can take more time for an immigrant to become a Permanent Resident than it does for a Permanent Resident to become a citizen.

There are many different ways to get your Permanent Resident visa, which is also called a "green card". This process can take from 0 – 25 years. Some special situations--like military service or marriage to a U.S. citizen--can shorten the time you need to wait for this visa.

__Step 2: Live in the United States, usually for 5 years.

After getting a green card, most people must live in the United States for 5 years before they can apply for citizenship. But there are exceptions to this. For example, if your spouse is an American citizen, you may become a citizen in 3 years. The time may also be much faster for immediate family members of U.S. citizens.

__Continuous residence (also see p. 19)

"Continuous residence" means that you have lived in the U.S. for a continuous length of time. You should not be outside of the U.S. longer than six months out of each year. Absence longer than six months can break your "continuous residence". You can travel outside the U.S. but you must be abroad for less than six months each year.

__Physical presence

This means that you need to be physically present in the U.S.— actually living in the U.S.—for 30 months within the 5 year period (or 18 months for spouses of citizens). Also, you must show USCIS that you have lived in your USCIS district or state for at least 3 months immediately before you filed the N-400 application. Exceptions can be made for some jobs. For eample, people working for the U.S. government, including the military, may be exempt.

Check with USCIS to see if you are eligible for an exception to the physical presence requirement. If you have an eligible employer, you must file Form N-470, "Application to Preserve Residence for Naturalization Purposes". (There is a $330 filing fee.)

When you complete steps 1-2 above, you are ready to apply for citizenship. Chapter 4 will tell you more details about this part of the application process. The steps below are a brief overview of what you will need to do next.

__Step 3: Complete Form N-400

__Step 4: Get 2 photos

__Step 5: Write your check

__Step 6: Mail your completed form N-400, and your check and photos, to your local USCIS Service Center.

__Step 7: Get Fingerprinted. After USCIS gets your application, they will tell you how to get fingerprinted.

__Step 8: Go to your appointment at the USCIS office.
You will be interviewed and be given a civics test orally and a test of basic reading and writing in English.

__Step 9: Your Results – Did you pass?

The USCIS officer tells you if you passed. If you did, USCIS will mail you a letter with the date of the citizenship ceremony.

__Step 10: Your Citizenship Ceremony!

You take the Oath of Citizenship and officially become a U.S. citizen.

Below: Immigrants serving in the U.S. military take the citizenship oath in a special ceremony at the White House (April 3, 2010)

President Obama is in the foreground. (White House Photo)

Continuous Residence: Most Frequently Asked Question

Question: "What should I do if I will be outside of the U.S. for six months or more?"

To the U.S. government, if you are outside of the United States 6 months or more, it shows USCIS that you do not think of the U.S. as your home and you have broken the residency requirement for naturalization.

If you give up your job and your home and take your family out of the country for six months or longer, USCIS can decide that you have given up your permanent residence in the U.S.. They will think you do not want to be a citizen and they will deny your application.

If this happens, you will have to start counting your "continuous residence" years again, starting with the year that you re-apply. (That will become Year #1).

Your "continuous residence" in the U.S. is very important. If you will be gone 6 months or longer, you should plan ahead. You can call USCIS before you leave and/or talk with an immigration lawyer about what you should do. They may tell you to apply for a Re-Entry Permit *before* you leave the U.S.

The continuous residency and physical presence requirements can be difficult to understand. Be sure that you read the information from USCIS about this important issue in Chapter 4. Information about the Re-entry Permit is on page 40.

Learning English

As you can see from Step 8 on the Citizenship Checklist on page 19, one of the most important things you can do to prepare for U.S. citizenship is to learn English. English will help you pass your citizenship test. Knowing English will also make your life in the United States so much easier.

Where Can I Learn English?

Some people learn English at work or from their English-speaking family members and friends. Some learn it from the radio, movies, television or computer-based media.

One of the most enjoyable and effective ways to learn English is to practice with other people. Community colleges, libraries, and local community organizations often have classes where you can practice speaking, reading and writing English with others. At an adult school, you can often find beginning, intermediate and advanced English classes. These classes are for adult students of all ages and nationalities.

Like adult schools, community colleges often have citizenship and English classes for foreign students. Community college classes are inexpensive and adult school classes may be free. You can often choose to go to these classes during the day or at night.

Frequent practice is important when you are learning a language. Practicing English with other foreign students and an experienced teacher can help you learn English better and faster.

These schools often have many different classes to help immigrants, including citizenship classes.

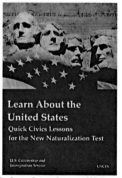

**Civics books will help
you prepare for citizenship.**

How to Find Adult School, Library and Community Center Classes

Adult schools are part of your local public school or community college system. You may be surprised to learn that Jill Biden, the wife of the current vice-president of the United States, teaches "English as a Second Language" (ESL) classes to foreign students at a community college in Virginia.

Community colleges are listed in your local phone book and on the computer. To find an adult school with English classes in your community, you can look online, in the phone book, or ask at your local library or high school. If you don't have a computer, you can use one for free at most neighborhood libraries. Libraries will also have free internet service.

You can also ask librarians for help with any of your questions. Like teachers, librarians are very knowledgable. They are glad to help you find the information that you need. You can also look online in the "Literacy Directory" at the website listed below. This is a United States government website that lists many English and citizenship classes throughout the country:

http://www.literacydirectory.org/

English as a Second Language — "ESL"

When you go to school to enroll, ask them for an "English as a Second Language" class. These are also called "ESL" classes. The abbreviation "ESL" is pronounced so that the name of each letter is said separately — "E" - "S" - "L". These classes may also be called "English as a Foreign Language" (EFL) classes.

Meeting People

It can be very lonely when you live in a new country far from your family and friends. Adult schools are excellent places to learn English and to prepare for citizenship. They are also good places to meet people in your neighborhood.

ESL students come from different backgrounds and ages. At an adult school, you may meet people from your own country. You may also meet people from other countries who know about the history and culture of your country and who also speak your language. At an adult school, you will meet many interesting people from all over the world. Many friendships begin in ESL classrooms.

For example, the parents of the current U.S. Secretary of Labor, Hilda Solis, met as adult students in a U.S. citizenship class. Her mother came to the United States from Nicaragua and her father came to the U.S. from Mexico.

Foreign students understand some of the difficulties of living in the U.S. better than many Americans do. Your classmates may be able to answer questions you have and tell about experiences that will help you. Churches, temples, mosques and other religious organizations can also help you meet people in your community. Sometimes they can also tell you how to get financial help or legal advice.

There are many places to learn English and many ways that you can practice it.

> *The more you speak English, the better you will speak. The more you read English, the better you will read. The more you write English, the better you will write.*

The most important thing you can do to become a citizen is to learn English. Your English will improve with practice, and you should look for ways to practice it often. This is important for your naturalization test and also because knowing English will make your life in the United States so much better.

3

How to Get a Permanent Resident Visa (Green Card)

Famous People in American History

George Washington
by Gilbert Stuart

Civics Test Question #69: Who is the "Father of Our Country?"

Answer: George Washington

Civics Test Question #70: Who was the first president of the United States?

Answer: George Washington

3

Getting a Permanent Resident Visa "Green Card"

The most important step in the citizenship process is to get your permanent resident visa (also called your "green card").

If you already have received your green card, congratulations! You have already done the hardest part of the citizenship process, and you should go on to read Chapter 4, "Applying for Citizenship".

What is a Green Card? The U.S. government gives this permanent resident visa to all immigrants who become legal permanent residents (LPRs) of the United States. This visa is often called a green card.

If you are a permanent resident age 18 or older, you must always have your green card with you. This card proves that you can legally live and work in the United States for as long as you want.

Expiration. Current green cards are valid for 10 years unless you are a conditional resident. Conditional green cards are only valid for 2 years. All green cards must be renewed before the card expires.

Other uses. When you complete Form I-9, "Employment Eligibility Verification", employers will see from your green card that you can legally work in the United States. It is also good identification when you apply for a Social Security Card or a state-issued driver's license.

A green card can be used for your readmission to the United States after a trip abroad IF you are not gone for longer than 1 year.

Green Card Requirements

What are the requirements to get a Green Card?

In general, to meet the requirements for a Green Card, you must:

1. Be eligible for one of the immigrant categories established in the Immigration and Nationality Act (see page 30) ;

2. Have a qualifying immigrant petition filed and approved for you;

3. File Form I-864 "Affadavit of Support". Petitioners must supply the I-864 Affidavit of Support showing that you have a source of support in the United States;

4. Have received a notification from USCIS that there is a visa available for you;

5. Be already in, or admissible to, the United States.

How the U.S. Gives Out Green Cards

Readers of this book are usually permanent residents who are now preparing for citizenship. But, for anyone who has questions about getting a green card, this chapter has a quick overview of the process.

Quotas by Country

USCIS limits the number of permanent resident visas they give out every year and they do not give the same number of visas to every country. The country you are from—and the number of visas that Congress allows to be given to people from that country—are two important parts of the green card process.

These visa quotas for countries often change. You can see the quota of visas for your country listed on the internet at:

www.usstatedept.gov

No limit. There is no limit on green cards for the husband, wife, parents or unmarried children of U.S. citizens. There is no waiting period for these applicants—just the required processing time. However, all other family-based categories usually have long waiting times.

Who Gets Visas First?

If you are in a family (non-immediate relative) or employment-based preference category, visa availability is determined by:

1. **Your country quota.** Different countries are allowed different numbers of permanent resident visas to be given to their citizens. If your country has many applicants and a small quota of visas allowed to it, you could be waiting many years for a green card.

2. **The USCIS preference in your immigration category.** Congress limits the number of visas given each year for most categories of immigrants. To get your green card, you must qualify in one of the categories set up by the U.S. Immigration and Nationality Act (see page 30).

3. **Your priority date.**

   A priority date will be assigned to you based on the date that you filed your immigrant petition with USCIS. USCIS compares this date with the date of other peoples' applications. For some jobs, the priority date may be based on the date the application for a labor certification was accepted by the Department of Labor. Your priority date holds your place on the list to get an immigrant visa.

How long will I wait? Do you have priority because of your application date? Have you waited longer than others in your category? The answers to these questions determine how long you will need to wait for your visa.

Categories of Eligible Immigrants

The most common ways to get a green card are in these categories, established by the U.S. Immigration and Nationality Act:

1. Relative of a U.S. citizen or permanent resident.
There are no limits on the number of green cards that USCIS gives to "immediate family" members.

Who is the **"Immediate Family"**? They are:

- Parents of a U.S. citizen
- Spouses of a U.S. citizen
- Unmarried children under the age of 21 of a U.S. citizen

2. Job. You have an employer who will hire you.

3. Investment.
You can apply for this visa if you are an entrepreneur with a large amount of money (usually $500,000 to $1,000,000) to spend on starting a business in the U.S..

4. Special skill or talent.
This category is often used for well-educated professionals, or performers or artists.

5. Refugee or Asylee.
You can get a visa as a refugee or if you need asylum.

6. Other. For other, less common, categories, see
www.uscis.gov

Steps to Getting a Green Card

Step 1: Identify your immigration category.

Step 2: Get a Sponsor.
Someone sponsors you, usually family or an employer .

Step 3: Petition.
Your sponsoor files a petition, including an affadavit of support.

Step 4: Approval.
USCIS approves your petition.

Step 5: Wait for a Visa.
You wait for a visa number to become available.

Step 6: File form I-485.
You file form I-485 "Application to Immigrate or Adjust Status"

Step 7: Adjust Status or have Consular Processing.
You follow the directions to get your visa if you are in the U.S. ("adjust status") or abroad (for "consular processing").

No limit. There is no limit on the number of immigrant visas available each year for some categories of people, including immediate relatives of U.S. citizens and special kinds of immigrants, including refugees. When the USCIS approves a refugee petition, the State Department will immediately give out an immigrant visa number. For more information on green card eligibility, see **www.uscis.gov.**

The "Diversity Lottery"
Another Way to Get a Green Card

You can see that it may take a long time to get your green card, if you are not sponsored by an immediate family member. But there is a special way to get a green card. The Diversity Immigrant Visa Program (DV) lets USCIS give out about 50,000 immigrant visas to people who were born in countries with low rates of immigration to the United States.

If your name is selected in this lottery, you can apply for permanent residence. You can also file for your spouse and any unmarried children under the age of 21. In 2012, fourteen million (14,000,000) people applied for a DV permanent resident card, but there were only 50,000 immigrant visa numbers available. As you can see, it is not easy to get a green card this way, but if you come from a country with low U.S. immigration, you may want to try.

Qualifying for a Diversity Immigrant Visa

If you get a diversity immigrant visa, you need to:

- complete an immigrant visa application,
- submit required documents and forms,
- pay required fees,
- complete a medical examination, and
- be interviewed by a consular officer at the U.S. embassy or consulate and show them that you are qualified.

During the visa interview, you must also:

- show proof of a high school education or its equivalent, OR
- show two years of work experience in the last five years. This must be "in an occupation that requires at least two years of training or experience."

Notification Letter. You should follow the instructions in your notification letter and complete everything they need.

Use it within 6 months. If you are told you won the Diversity Lottery, you and your family can receive an immigrant visa in your passport(s). You need to "activate" this visa within six months by showing your passport at any port of entry to the United States.

As a new immigrant, your passport will be stamped with the visa to show you can legally live and work in the U.S.. In a few months, USCIS will mail you your green card. (If you are in the US already, you can apply for an adjustment of status instead.)

Ineligible Immigrants. Due to their high immigration numbers, immigrants from the following countries were not eligible to participate in the Diversity Visa Lottery in 2012: Brazil, Canada, China (mainland-born, excluding Hong Kong S.A.R. and Taiwan), Colombia, Dominican Republic, Ecuador, El Salvador, Guatemala, Haiti, India, Jamaica, Mexico, Pakistan, Peru, the Philippines, Poland, South Korea, United Kingdom (except Northern Ireland) and its dependent territories, and Vietnam.

For more information, always check the Diversity Lottery website: `http://travel.state.gov/visa/immigrants/types/type s_1318.html`

Beware of Fraud and Scams

The Office of Visa Services at the Department of State often warns immigrants about false emails and letters that are sometimes sent to applicants for the Diversity Immigrant Visa (DV) Lottery Program. Ignore these. Do not listen to people who contact you and ask you to pay them because they represent the U.S. government. They are not telling you the truth.

Never pay anyone to give you information about your status in the Diversity Lottery (DV). You can find out for free if you were selected for DV processing. USCIS will never ask you for a payment online. They will only ask for money to be paid (1) in person in a government office, or (2) with a check that you mail to an official government address.

Payment. Fees for the DV application process are paid directly to the United States embassy or consulate cashier when you go to your scheduled appointment. The U.S. government will never ask you to send payment for the Diversity Visa (DV) before that time.

How to Check Your DV Status Online. Go to the Kentucky Consular Center website of the State Department to check your Entrant Status for free:

http://www.dvlottery.state.gov

Note on Translations: The only official translation of the Diversity Lottery Visa requirements is in English, on the State Department website. There are other languages linked there, but the State Department only verifies that the English translation is correct.

Conditional Residence: Removing Conditions

If you apply for permanent residence because you recently married a US citizen or if you apply as an investor, USCIS will give you conditional permanent residence for two years. The expiration date of the conditional period is two years from the approval date. The immigrant visa category is CR (conditional resident).

Conditions due to Marriage. You may have a conditional visa because you married a U.S. citizen. When you apply for the removal of these conditions, you will need to give USCIS evidence that your marriage was not fraudulent. Examples of evidence would be a marriage certificate, birth certificates of children, joint financial statements, and letters from employers, friends and relatives.

If the evidence that you submit is not strong enough, an immigration official may ask to have a follow-up interview. Under most circumstances, the husband and wife must both go to this interview.

Conditions due to Investment. If you became a conditional permanent resident because of your investments, you need to file form I-829 "Petition by Entrepreneur to Remove Conditions". Once your application is received, USCIS will extend your permanent residence visa every year until conditions are removed or denied.

Getting rid of a Conditional Requirement

When USCIS approves your request to remove a conditional requirement, you will receive an I-551 stamp in your passport. Your new Permanent Resident Card will come to your home in the mail in several weeks or in several months. It replaces your old two-year conditional residence card.

Conditional Residence and the Citizenship Requirement

It is important to know that the two-year conditional residence period counts toward your citizenship residency requirement. USCIS must remove your conditional residency first. After that, you may submit a separate citizenship/naturalization application to USCIS.

How to Change Your Visa Status

How to change your visa status if you live in the U.S.

Adjustment of Status

You apply differently for a permanent resident visa if you are living inside or outside of the United States. If you are in the U.S. with a visa and you want a green card, you need to change the status of your current visa. This is called an "Adjustment of Status". You do not need to go back to your home country to apply for it.

Form I-485, "Application to Register Permanent Resident or Adjust Status". You need to file this form and stay in the United States until your I-485 application is approved. USCIS says that you do not need to worry if your Form I-94 visa expires during this time. You can still stay in the United States while your application is processed.

USCIS will tell you if your petition (application) is approved and when your immigrant visa number is ready. They will tell you when to send them more information and when to send them your visa processing fees. When your visa change is approved, they will mail you your green card.

How to change your visa status if you live outside of the U.S.

Consular Processing

If you live outside of the U.S. you need to apply for a green card through a U.S. consulate or embassy before you come to the United States. This is called "Consular Processing".

If you are approved, USCIS will send the approved petition to the Department of State's National Visa Center (NVC), where it will wait for you until an immigrant visa number is available.

The National Visa Center will tell you when the visa petition is received. They will tell you when to send visa processing fees and when you need to send them more information. They will also tell you when your immigrant visa number is available.

How to Find Out the Status of Your Application

You may check the status of your application online. Look at "My Case Status" at the website below:

`https://egov.uscis.gov/cris/Dashboard/CaseStatus.do`

Please remember that an e-filed receipt number may not be available at the website above through "My Case Status" for 72 hours. If you have any questions, you can call the USCIS National Customer Service Center at 1-800-375-5283. Be ready to give them information about your application. They will want to know your name, date of birth, receipt number, and Alien Registration Number.

When to Renew a Green Card

Form I-551. A Permanent Resident Card (USCIS Form I-551) is proof of your permanent resident status in the United States. Some kinds of green cards do not have an expiration date, but most are given to immigrants for 10 years and then must be renewed.

Form I-90. You should renew your green card if you are a permanent resident and your card is either already expired or it will expire within the next 6 months. Renew it with Form I-90.

How to Appeal if Your Application is Denied

If your application to renew your green card is denied, you will receive a letter with the explanation. If you receive a negative decision, you may submit a written request to reopen or reconsider your application. Send it to the same office that denied you.

In your request, you must show that the decision to deny your application was based on incorrect application of law or immigration policy. You can show that the decision was incorrect based on the evidence already in your file. Or you can submit new evidence. (See "How Do I Appeal the Denial of Petition or Application?" at www.uscis.gov.)

Losing Permanent Resident Status

Your permanent resident card can be taken from you for many reasons. For example, it can be taken away if you commit a crime. You may also lose your green card if you do not file your income tax. And you can lose your permanent resident status if your green card application was fraudulent (untrue).

You do not want to stay outside the USA for more than 365 days because it will look like you don't live there any more. Consider getting a re-entry permit before leaving the country for a long time.

Getting Help

If you need advice, contact the USCIS District Office near your home for a list of organizations that may be able to help you to prepare your application. To locate the office serving your area, go to www.uscis.gov. Look in the section called, "Find a USCIS Office".

Permanent Resident Card
"Green Card"

The permanent resident card is an identification card. It shows that you are legally a permanent resident of the United States. If you have a green card you can live and work in the United States forever. You do not need to become a U.S. citizen.

The permanent resident card is made of plastic and is the size of a credit card. It has your name and photograph and your Alien ID number ("A" number). It used to be green, then was white, then was redesigned in 2010 and is now green again. The new green card also has new security features: holographic images, laser-engraved fingerprints, and high resolution micro-images. It is now difficult to make Illegal copies of the green card and it is easy to catch a forgery.

Your green card can be taken away if you commit a serious crime or if you are outside the United States longer than the law allows.

The permanent resident card or green card, is also called a Form I-551. After the terrorist attack on September 11, 2001, it became more important for permanent residents to always carry their green card with them. The U.S. Department of Homeland Security (DHS) can ask to see it at any time.

Citizenship Residency Requirement

Most permanent residents can apply for citizenship (naturalization) after five years of residency. If you became a permanent resident through asylum, you need four years of residency before you can become a citizen. If you married a U.S. citizen, you only need three years of residency before you can apply.

If you have had a conditional permanent resident visa for two years because you married a U.S. citizen, you can use those two years toward your citizenship requirement. Permanent residents may submit their applications for naturalization as early as 90 days before meeting the residency requirement.

When You Have a Green Card You Must...

Maintain Permanent Resident Status

The card holder must keep permanent resident status. You can be removed from the United States if you do not keep this status.

Always Have Your Green Card With You

The Immigration and Nationality Act says that permanent residents eighteen years of age or older must carry their green card at all times. If you do not do this, there may be a penalty fee of $100 and/or imprisonment for up to 30 days. Only the federal government can give these penalties.

Register for Military Service. Male permanent residents between the ages of 18 and 26 need to register in the Selective Service System (U.S. military).

Pay Taxes. Permanent residents who live in the US must pay taxes on their worldwide income, just like US citizens.

Re-entry Permit

Question: "What form do I need if I am going to be out of the United States longer than my green card allows?"

Answer: Re-entry Permit Form I-131.

If you think you will be out of the U.S. for more than 12 months you should apply for a re-entry permit before leaving the country. You should file Form I-131, "Application for a Travel Document". You can get this form at `http://www.uscis.gov` or by calling 1-800-870-3676. You must pay a fee to file Form I-131. (See page 42).

In most cases, none of the time you were in the United States before you left the country will count toward your time in continuous residence.

This means that you will need to begin your continuous residence again after you return to the United States, and you may have to wait up to four years and one day before you can apply for naturalization.

A re-entry permit is valid for up to two years. You may show a re-entry permit instead of your permanent resident card at a port of entry (if you have been gone for less than 12 months) or instead of a visa (if you have been gone for more than 12 months) when you return to the United States after a temporary absence.

Having a re-entry permit does not guarantee that you will be admitted to the United States when you return, but it can make it easier to show that you are returning from a temporary visit abroad.

Go to `http://www.statedept.gov` or your nearest Department of State consular office overseas for more information.

Question: Do I need a Reentry Permit (Form I-131)? Or do I need an "Application to Preserve Residence for Naturalization Purposes" (Form N-470) ?

A re-entry permit (Form I-131) and the "Application to Preserve Residence for Naturalization Purposes" (Form N-470) are not the same. Form N-470 is for a permanent resident who must leave the U.S. for employment purposes and still plans to naturalize.

 Review: "What should I do if I was out of the U.S. longer than my green card allows?"

You need to renew your PR (permanent resident visa) abroad. Go to the state department's website below and follow their instructions.

```
http://travel.state.gov/visa/immigrants/info/
                info_1333.html
```

 Review: 5 Important Things You Need To Do To Become a U.S. Citizen

1. Get a valid permanent resident visa

2. Keep a "physical presence" in the US .
"Physical presence" means that you have physically lived in the United States for at least half the time that is required for your citizenship residency requirement.

3. Keep a continuous residency in the U.S..
For most people the continuous residency requirement is 5 years. See pages 18, 20 and 52, for more information.

4. Mail your application with 2 photos and a check.

5. Pass your citizenship interview and tests.

Cost of Filing Common Immigration Forms

Name of the Form	Number	Fee	Biometrics
Alien's Change of Address Card	AR-11	None	N/A
Application to Replace Permanent Resident Card	I-90	$366*	N/A
Petition for Alien Relative	I-130	$420	N/A
Application for Travel Document (re-entry permit)	I-131	See Special Instructions	
Petition for Alien Worker	I-140	$580	N/A
Application for Advance Permission to Return to Unrelinquished Domicile	I-191	$585	$85
Immigrant Petition by Alien Entrepreneur	I-526	$1500	N/A
Intending Immigrant's Affadavit of Support Exemption	I-864W	*see below	
Refugee/Asylee Petition	I-750	None	N/A
Petition to Remove the Conditions of Residence (below)	I-751	$505	N/A
Application for Employment Authorization	I-765	$380	N/A
Petition by Entrepreneur to Remove Conditions	I-829	$3,750	$85

An additional biometric services fee of $85 must be paid for each conditional resident dependent, listed under Part 3 or Part 4 of Form I-829

Name of the Form	Number	Fee	Biometrics
Affadavit of Support Under Section 213A of the Act	I-864	*see below	
Affadavit of Support Under Section 213A of the Act	I-864EZ	*see below	
Request for Fee Waiver	I-912	None	N/A

* Although USCIS does not charge a fee for this form, the Department of State does charge a fee when the Affidavit of Support is reviewed domestically. This does not apply when the Affidavit of Support is filed abroad..

Cost of Filing Common Immigration Forms

Name of the Form	Number	Fee	Biometrics
Application to File Declaration of Intent	N-300	$250	N/A
Application for Naturalization	N-400	$595*	$85
Request for Certification of Military or Naval Service	N-426	None	N/A
Application to Preserve Residence for Naturalization Purposes	N-470	$305	N/A
Application for Replacement of Naturalization/Citizenship Documents	N-565	$345	N/A
Application for Certificate of Citizenship	N-600	$600	N/A
Medical Certification for Disability Exceptions	N-648	None	N/A

To check for any changes in fees go to http://www.uscis.gov/fees. Or call USCIS National Customer Service Center at 1-800-375-5283 and ask for the fee information.

From USCIS: Fee Waiver for Certain Forms and Services

You may apply for a fee waiver for some immigration benefits and services if you cannot afford to pay. Go online for a complete list of forms and services that are eligible for a fee waiver at:

http://www.uscis.gov/feewaiver

The review of any fee waiver request will follow a series of steps beginning with determining whether the applicant is receiving a means-tested benefit, or analyzing whether the applicant's household income level and/or recent financial hardship makes him or her eligible for the fee waiver. USCIS will decide if your finances make you eligible.

NOTE: Granting of a fee waiver is at the sole discretion of USCIS.

4

Applying for Citizenship: An Overview

Famous People in American History

Benjamin Franklin
by Joseph Siffred Duplessis

Civics Question #68: What is one thing Benjamin Franklin is famous for?

Answer: He was (1) a diplomat, (2) the first postmaster; and (3) started the first free library.

4

Applying for Citizenship: An Overview

U.S. citizens have many rights that permanent residents don't have.

"What are some rights of U.S. citizens?"

As a U.S. citizen you can....

- bring relatives to the United States to become citizens;
- leave the United States for as long as you want and easily come back;
- work for the U.S. government;
- be protected from deportation in most cases;
- get government benefits and other public help (financial or medical);
- vote;
- hold some government elected offices (naturalized citizens cannot become President);
- have the protection of a U.S. passport and the help of the U.S. government when you travel abroad.

The most difficult part of becoming a U.S. citizen is getting your Green Card (permanent resident visa). After that important step, you need to meet the USCIS requirements and file your N-400 form to apply for citizenship. Chapter 3 explained how you can get and keep a green card. Chapter 4 gives you information about each of the steps to citizenship.

Citizens have more rights and responsibilities than permanent residents. Permanent residents cannot vote, they cannot compete in federal and state elections, and they cannot work for the federal government. It is very difficult—and it can take a long time—for permanent residents to sponsor their family members to become U.S. citizens. It is much faster to sponsor your family after you have become a U.S. citizen.

Guides for Immigrants: Living in the U.S.

There are not many requirements for citizenship-naturalization, and it is important to know exactly what USCIS requires. For that reason, much of the information in this section, "Requirements for Naturalization", is exactly as it is written by the USCIS.

[Publisher's Note: This information is also available in a readable new edition of this USCIS information by Lakewood Publishing, *Guide for New Immigrants: Welcome to the United States*. You can also get our USCIS Spanish edition, *Guía para inmigrantes nuevos: Bienvenidos a los Estados Unidos de América:*]

You can check the following websites for information about these English or Spanish guidesbooks to life in the U.S. for immigrants:

**www.welcomeesl.com and
www.lakewoodpublishing.com**

The 6 general requirements for naturalization are listed below. There is more detail about each of these requirements on the pages that follow this list.

6 Requirements for Naturalization

1. Live in the U.S. as a permanent resident for a specific amount of time **(Continuous Residence)**.

2. Be present in the U.S. for specific time periods **(Physical Presence)**.

3. Spend specific amounts of time in your state or USCIS district **(Time in State or USCIS District)**.

4. Behave in a legal and acceptable manner **(Good Moral Character)**.

5. Know English and information about U.S. history and government **(English and Civics)**.

6. Understand and accept the principles of the U.S. Constitution **(Attachment to the Constitution)**.

1. Continuous Residence

As explained in Chapter 3, "continuous residence" means that you must live in the U.S. as a permanent resident for a certain period of time. Most people must be permanent residents in continuous residence for five years (or three years if they are married to a U.S. citizen) before they can apply for naturalization.

For refugees, this means five years from the date you arrived in the U.S., which is usually the date you obtained permanent resident status. For those who have been given asylum status in the U.S., this period begins one year before you got permanent resident status.

The date on your Permanent Resident Card is the date your five years begins. If you leave the United States for a long period of time, usually more than six months, you may "break" your continuous residence.

Preserving Your Residence for Naturalization Purposes: Exemptions for One-Year Absences

If you work for the U.S. government, a recognized U.S. research institution, or certain U.S. corporations, or if you are a member of the clergy serving abroad, you may be able to preserve your continuous residence if you:

(1) **Have been physically present** and living in the U.S. without leaving for at least one year after becoming a permanent resident.

(2) **Submit Form N-470**, "Application to Preserve Residence for Naturalization Purposes", before you have been outside the U.S. for one year. There is a fee to file Form N-470 (see page 43).

USCIS Forms Phone Number

For more information, contact the USCIS Forms Line at:
1-800-870-3676
and ask for *Form N-470*, "Application to Preserve Residence for Naturalization Purposes".
You can also get the form on the USCIS website at:
http://www.uscis.gov

Tip: If you are outside of the United States while your naturalization application is in progress, it could cause problems with your eligibility, especially if you accept employment abroad.

Exemptions for Military Personnel (Form N-426)

If you are on active-duty status or were recently discharged from the U.S. Armed Forces, the continuous residence and physical presence requirements may not apply to you.

You can find more information in the M-599 "Naturalization Information for Military Personnel" brochure.

Every military base should have a point-of-contact to handle your naturalization application and certify a Form N-426.

Request for a "Certification of Military or Naval Service".
You must submit Form N-426 with your application forms.

U.S. Military Helpline

To get the forms you need, call the USCIS toll-free Military Help Line at: `1-877-CIS-4MIL` (1-877-247-4645).

You can find more information at `http://www.uscis.gov/military` or by calling Customer Service at `1-800-375-5283`.

---

2. Physical Presence in the United States

"Physical presence" means that you have been living in the United States, not living outside of the country.

If you are a permanent resident at least 18 years old, you must be living in the United States—"physically present"--for at least 30 months during the last five years before you apply for naturalization.

Married to a U.S. citizen. If you are married to a U.S. citizen, you must be physically present for at least 18 months during the last three years before you can apply for naturalization.

Question: What is the difference between *physical presence* presence and *continuous residence*?

Answer: "Physical presence" is the total number of days that you were inside the United States and does not include the time you spent outside of the U.S. Each day you spend outside of the United States takes away from your total days of physical presence.

If you are away from the U.S. for long periods of time or if you take many short trips outside of the U.S., you may not be able to meet your physical presence requirement.

To count your physical presence time, you should add together all the time you have been in the United States. Then subtract all trips you have taken outside the United States.

This includes short trips to Canada and Mexico. For example, if you go to Mexico for a weekend, you must include that trip when you count how many days you have spent out of the country.

"Continuous residence" is the total time you have lived as a permanent resident in the United States before applying for naturalization. If you spend too much time outside the United States during a single trip, you may break your continuous residence.

3. Time as a Resident in State or USCIS District

Most people must live in the state or USCIS district where they apply for naturalization for at least three months. Students can apply for naturalization either where they go to school or where their family lives (if they depend on their parents for support).

4. Good Moral Character

To be eligible for naturalization, you must be a person of good moral character.

A person is not considered to be of "good moral character" if they commit certain crimes during the five years before they apply for naturalization or if they lie during their naturalization interview.

Actions That Might Show a Lack of Good Moral Character

- Drunk driving or being drunk most of the time.
- Illegal gambling.
- Prostitution.
- Lying to gain immigration benefits.
- Failing to pay court-ordered child support.
- Committing terrorist acts.
- Persecuting someone because of race, religion, national origin, political opinion, or social group.

If you commit some specific crimes, you can never become a U.S. citizen and will probably be removed from the country. These crimes are called "bars" to naturalization.

Permanent Bars to Naturalization. You can be permanently barred from citizenship if you commit a serious crime called an "aggravated felony", on or after November 29, 1990. These include: murder, rape, sexual abuse of a child, violent assault, treason, and illegal trafficking in drugs, firearms or people.

Immigrants who deserted from the U.S. Armed Forces, are also permanently barred from U.S. citizenship.

You also may be denied citizenship if you behave in other ways that show you lack good moral character. Look at **www.uscis.gov** for the complete list.

Temporary Bars to Naturalization. Other crimes are temporary bars to naturalization. Temporary bars usually prevent you from becoming a citizen for up to five years after you commit the crime.

These temporary bars to naturalization may include:

- Any crime against a person with intent to harm.
- Any crime against property or the government involving fraud.
- Two or more crimes with combined sentences of five years or more.
- Violating controlled substance laws (e.g., using or selling illegal drugs).
- Spending 180 days or more during the past five years in jail or prison.

You must tell USCIS if you have committed any crime. When you apply for naturalization, report any crimes that you have committed. This includes crimes that were removed from your record or committed before your 18th birthday.

If you do not tell USCIS about crimes in your past, you may be denied citizenship and you could be prosecuted.

5. English and Civics

In general, you must show that you can read, write, and speak basic English. You also must have a basic knowledge of U.S. history and government (also known as "civics"). You will be required to pass a test of English and a test of civics to prove your knowledge.

Many schools and community organizations help people prepare for their citizenship tests. You can find examples of test questions in *A Guide to Naturalization*.

6. Attachment to the Constitution

You must be willing to support and defend the United States and its Constitution. You declare your "attachment"—meaning that you promise to be loyal to the United States and the Constitution—when you take the Oath of Allegiance (see page 102).

People who show they have a physical or developmental disability that makes them unable to understand the meaning of the Oath do not have to take the Oath of Allegiance.

Change of Address. If you have a naturalization application in progress with USCIS and you move, you must tell USCIS your new address.

To Report a Change of Address

You can call 1-800-375-5283 to report your new address. You must also file Form AR-11 with DHS.

You may change your address online via an electronic Form AR-11 at `http://www.uscis.gov`

Naturalization Ceremony

If USCIS approves your N-400 application at your citizenship interview, they will invite you to the naturalization ceremony and you will take the Oath of Allegiance there. You are not officially a citizen until you have taken the Oath of Allegiance. The Oath of Allegiance ceremony is a public event.

"Notice of Naturalization Oath Ceremony" (Form N-445)

USCIS will send you a Form N-445, "Notice of Naturalization Oath Ceremony", to tell you the time and date of your naturalization ceremony. You must complete this form and bring it to the ceremony.

Rescheduling

If you cannot go to your ceremony, you can reschedule it. To reschedule, you must return Form N-445 to your local USCIS office and include a letter where you explain the reason that you cannot attend.

The Oath Ceremony

On the day of the naturalization ceremony, you will return your permanent resident card to USCIS. They will give every new citizen a "Certificate of Naturalization" instead.

At the naturalization ceremony an official will read each part of the Oath of Allegiance slowly and ask you to repeat the words.

After you take the oath, you will receive your Certificate of Naturalization. This certificate proves that you are a U.S. citizen.

**Review**
Citizenship Checklist:

**"I've completed all of the USCIS naturalization
requirements. What should I do now?"**

__Step 1. Complete Form N-400.

Permanent Residents use an N-400 form to apply for citzen-
ship (naturalization). Links to this form are available at:
www.welcomeesl.com or **www.uscis.gov**

__Step 2. Get Photos.

Get 2 photos for your application. Passport-style photos are
good.

__Step 3. Write a check or get a money order from the bank.

For most people, the cost of applying for citizenship is now
$680 ($595 for your application fee and $85 for fingerprints.)
Look on the USCIS website for any changes.

USCIS will tell you to get fingerprints after USCIS receives
your check. (Send one check for the total of $680, not two
separate checks).

Make your check payable to:
U.S. Department of Homeland Security

To find the correct mailing address for your area, see the
service centers listed on pages 60-62.

__Step 4. Get an envelope. You should put inside it:

___ **a letter*** with your **name** and the your eight digit **Alien "A" number** on your green card and a list of the **documents** you are including.

*If it is difficult to write a letter, you can fill in the letter that follows page 62 in this book. Remove the page from this book and write in your information. Then mail that letter in an envelope together with everything you need to include from this checklist.

___ **a photocopy of your green card.** Photocopy the front and back of your green card separately so you will have two separate sheets of regular letter size photocopy paper. Send both papers. Don't cut the photocopy to be the size of the card.

___ **Form N-400**. Complete it, but do NOT sign it*.

___ **Check or Money Order** for your N-400 Application and Fingerprint fees (currently $680).

___ **And any extra documents**

Include any other **photocopied documents** you need to send to the USCIS (especially if you have any problems. For example, USCIS might need to see your marriage license, divorce decree or birth certificate.)

___ **Step 5. Mail it.** Mail your completed form N-400, and your check and photos, to your local USCIS Service Center.

The service centers are listed on page 60-62. You can also call USCIS with questions at:

1-800-375-5283 or
1-800-767-1833 (TTY) – for the hearing impaired

___ Step 6. Get Fingerprinted

USCIS will send you an appointment letter after they receive your application, photos and payment. When you get the USCIS appointment letter, follow their directions and get fingerprinted.

___ Step 7. Go to your appointment with the USCIS. Bring everything you need.

Be on time for your appointment. Have everything you need, especially if there are documents the USCIS wants to see (for example, a marriage or birth certificate). You will be interviewed at a USCIS office.

The USCIS officer will want to know that your information is honest and that you have the qualities of a good citizen. You will be given opportunities to show that you can read, speak and write English and answer civics questions. (For some exceptions to this, see Chapter 6).

___ Step 8: Your Results

The USCIS officer tells you if you passed. (If you didn't, you can take the part that you didn't pass on another day.)

___ Step 9: USCIS sends you a letter

When you pass, sometimes you will be given the citizenship oath on the same day, in the USCIS office. But usually the USCIS officer will tell you that you passed and you will get a letter in the mail later. This letter will tell you the date and time for your citizenship ceremony.

If you did not pass, USCIS will mail you a letter explaining when you can come back and re-test the parts that you missed. But you will probably pass the first time.

___ Step 10: Your Citizenship Ceremony!

Sometimes you will be given the citizenship oath on the day you pass your citizenship test. But usually there will be a ceremony with it.

Sometimes it is a small ceremony. But if you live near a large city, there may be hundreds of other immigrants taking the citizenship oath with you. Family members usually wait outside, but there is a lot of excitement both inside and outside the room on that day. After you take your oath, you are now officially a U.S. Citizen!

"Where Should I Mail My Citizenship Application?"

Regional Service Centers

Mail your application with your 2 photos and any other documents to the USCIS Regional Service Center that serves the state where you live. You can find your center on the lists below.

1. If you live in Alaska, Arizona, California, Colorado, Hawaii, Idaho, Illinois, Indiana, Iowa, Kansas, Michigan, Minnesota, Missouri, Montana, Nebraska, Nevada, North Dakota, Ohio, Oregon, South Dakota, Utah, Washington, Wisconsin, Wyoming, Territory of Guam, or the Commonwealth of the Northern Mariana Islands, send your application to:

USCIS
P.O. Box 21251
Phoenix, AZ 85036

For Express Mail or courier deliveries, use the following address:

USCIS
Attn: N-400
1820 E. Skyharbor Circle S
Suite 100
Phoenix, AZ 85034

2. If you live in Alabama, Arkansas, Connecticut, Delaware, District of Columbia, Florida, Georgia, Kentucky, Louisiana, Maine, Maryland, Massachusetts, Mississippi, New Hampshire, New Jersey, New Mexico, New York, North Carolina, Oklahoma, Pennsylvania, Rhode Island, South Carolina, Tennessee, Texas, Vermont, Virginia, West Virginia, Commonwealth of Puerto Rico, or the U.S. Virgin Islands, send your application to:

USCIS
P.O. Box 660060
Dallas, TX 75266

For Express Mail or courier deliveries, use the following address:

USCIS
Attn: N-400
2501 S State Hwy 121 Business
Suite 400
Lewisville, TX 75067

3. **Military.** For applications from current or former members of the military, spouses of current members of the military, and close relatives of deceased members of the military:

Send your application to the Nebraska Service Center (NSC) regardless of where you live and whether you are filing from within the United States or abroad.

Nebraska Service Center
P.O. Box 87426
Lincoln, NE 68501-7426

For Express Mail or courier deliveries, use the following address:

Nebraska Service Center
850 S. Street
Lincoln, NE 68508

Remember: Include a Letter
with Your Application

You should send a short letter to USCIS with your name on it and a list of what is in the envelope when you send them your application. It is a good idea to send a letter like this—called a "cover letter" every time you write USCIS. It will help them understand what you need.

If you do not want to write a letter, you can remove the blank letter on the next page. Then you can write in your own information on it and mail it to USCIS. Send it together with your Form N-400 application, in the same envelope.

You can also call USCIS for the addresses at 1-800-375-5283 or 1-800-767-1833 (TTY)—for the hearing impaired.

To: USCIS

Date:

My name is _____

Address: _____

City, State: _____

My Alien ("A") number is _____

I am including my N-400 form and a photocopy of the front and back of my green card. I have also included my check or money order for $_____.

If I need to send other documents, I have listed them in the space below.
Thank you for your help.

Signature _____

If I have included any extra documents or information with my application they are listed on the lines below:

_____

_____

_____

_____

_____

_____

_____

_____

Review

Remember: When you mail your application....

- **Complete the N-400 form. Use a blue or black ink pen and print very neatly.**
  Or you can use a computer to type it. Or go online to complete your application and print it on your printer.

- **Make copies.**
  Make and keep a copy of your completed N-400 application and all the other papers you send to USCIS.

  If they don't need the original papers, send copies. You can bring the original documents with you to your interview.

- **Mail it**.
  Mail the envelope at the Post Office. At the post office, ask them to send your envelope "Certified Mail, Return Receipt Requested".

- **Certified Mail**
  Certified mail costs a little more, but you will get a paper sent back to you after your envelope is delivered. This proves that USCIS received your envelope. Save this paper.

Remember: USCIS gets many, many papers from immigrants, and some-times documents can be lost. Don't send anything to USCIS that you want to get back. If they do not need the original documents, send them a copy. If they need to have the ori-ginal document, remember to keep copies of everything that you send them.

Review

What happens after you mail your N-400 application form, check, and photos?

1. Get Fingerprinted ("biometrics"). USCIS will write back and tell you to get fingerprints taken.

2. Go to your scheduled appointment. USCIS will give you an appointment time for your citizenship interview and tests.

3. The Interview. You will go to your appointment with USCIS for your citizenship interview and tests.

When you are interviewed, the USCIS officer wants to know that your information is honest and that you have the qualities of a good citizen.

You will also show the USCIS officer that you can read, speak and write basic English and that you know about U.S. government and history (civics). The next chapter will explain the four parts of the citizenship test and what you need to do to pass them. Chapter 8 will have more detailed information about this. Chapter 9 will give you practice with possible interview questions. The chapters that follow will help you prepare for all the other parts of the citizenship test.

For exceptions to the USCIS naturalization requirements, see Chapter 6. For more information, to get help or to find government resources, see Chapter 7.

5

The Citizenship Test
"What Do I Need to Know?"

Famous People in American History

Thomas Jefferson
by Randolph Peale

Civics Test Question #62: Who wrote the Declaration of Independence?

Answer: Thomas Jefferson

5

The Citizenship Test

"What Do I Need to Know for My Citizenship Test?"

The USCIS Officer

The person who interviews and tests you represents USCIS. He is called an "officer". The USCIS officer is employed by the U.S. government. He is not with the police or other law enforcement agencies.

The USCIS officer will have your application and all of your paperwork. He (or she) will ask many questions about your N-400 application. This is a normal part of the citizenship interview.

When you go to the citizenship interview, usually only one person will interview you for all 4 parts of it.

But sometimes one person will ask the N-400 questions and then a different person will ask questions about civics and English. This is also normal.

Answering these questions is a good opportunity for you. When you answer, you show the interviewer that you are honest, will be a good citizen, and that you can understand and speak English.

Do not worry about your accent or grammar as long as you can be understood. Speak slowly if you need to. If you don't understand a question, you can ask the interviewer to repeat it. You can say, "Could you please repeat that?"

The USCIS officer will be glad to repeat a question for you, if you ask him to do that.

Four Parts to the Citizenship Test

There are four (4) parts to your Citizenship-Naturalization Test. The test practices in this book begin with Chapter 8 in Section 3. Many people do not know what to expect at their citizenship interview. Section 3 has many practices for all parts of the citizenship interview and tests. It lets you practice the skills that you will need, including opportunites to read and write English.

Practice your answers to interview questions.

Citizenship Test, Part 1
Talking to the USCIS Officer About Yourself

You need to send USCIS an application form when you want to apply to become a citizen. This is the N-400 application form.

At your citizenship interview, the USCIS officer will ask you many questions. USCIS does not tell these questions in advance, but many of them will be about the information on your N-400 application form.

Be sure that you know your N-400 information well. If there are problems, or answers that you need to explain, bring all of the documents you need with you to your interview. (Some examples of papers to bring would be marriage, divorce or birth documents or court records of convictions).

Interview Practices

In Chapter 9 you will read and practice interviews. Your interview is the part that will take the most time in the USCIS office. In this chapter you will practice answering possible questions from USCIS.

It is very important for you to know the information on your N-400 form and to be able to talk about it for your interview. The USCIS interviewer will ask questions about your life, your work and your reasons for wanting to become a U.S. citizen.

The USCIS officer will ask these questions to decide if (1) your N-400 information is true, and (2) you are able to understand and speak English. Most people are nervous about this part, but they pass.

This book includes questions and answers that you can practice for your interview. You should read, write and speak the answers already written in this book and also write, read and say your own answers.

There is also a link to an example of a USCIS interview that you can watch online at: **www.welcomeesl.com.**

Citizenship Test, Part 2
Reading an English Sentence

The USCIS officer will ask you to read 1-3 sentences in English. When you read one of these sentences correctly, you have passed the reading test and you do not need to read any more.

Citizenship Test, Part 3
Writing an English Sentence

The USCIS interviewer will read 1-3 sentences to you and you will write them down. When you write one of them correctly, you pass the writing test and you will not need to write any more.

Reading and Writing Practice:
USCIS Vocabulary and Sentences

USCIS does not publish the words that they use for the citizenship reading and writing tests. But they do list words that they think you should know. Chapters 10 and 11 have many helpful reading, writing and vocabulary practices, including the two lists of words that USCIS recommends.

Chapter 12 lets you practice reading and writing the 500 most common words in English. These are the words Americans use most frequently. In chapter 13, you can read and write many sentences.

Practice Alone or With a Partner

All of the reading and writing activities in this book can be practiced alone or with a partner. Practicing with a partner (a friend, classmate, or family member) can be very helpful. She can read words and sentences out loud to you while you write the words and sentences down. (Reading aloud like this to someone who writes down what you read to them is called "giving dictation").

Practice, practice, practice!

The reading and writing practices in this book will help you prepare for the citizenship tests in English. You should also look for other opportunities to read, write and speak English often.

Writing in a Notebook or Journal Every Day

Many people find that writing in a notebook every day is good writing practice. This is true even if you only write one or two sentences a day. Even writing down new or difficult words you have seen or heard is a good activity. If you look up these new words in a dictionary you can improve your reading, writing and vocabulary.

When you copy these definitions and sample sentences into a notebook, it is another good way to practice English.

The more you practice reading, writing and speaking English, the easier the citizenship test will be for you.

Adult schools help many people learn English

Citizenship Test, Part 4
Civics Questions

The study of the history, government and culture of a country is called "civics". To pass the U.S. civics test, you need to correctly answer 6 of the 10 questions from the official USCIS list of civics questions.

The USCIS website shows all of the 100 questions and answers that they want you to know for the civics test. The USCIS interviewer will ask you 6 - 10 questions from this list of 100 questions. You can see them all in Chapter 14.

Chapter 15 lets you practice civics test questions with multiple choice answers. This book includes multiple choice civics tests because they are a good way to review the information

But remember that the civics test is an oral test. You will <u>not</u> be asked to read or write any of the answers.

All of the questions the USCIS officer asks you about civics will be oral and you will answer orally, too.

Different Ways to Practice the Civics Questions

Civics questions can be practiced in many different ways. This book has civics questions as:

(1) questions and answers (Chapter 14, p.225):

(2) multiple choice quizzes (Chapter 15, p.251)

(3) civics questions only—no answers (Chapter 16, p.277)

(4) questions for people 65 years and older (Chapter 17, p.287)

(5) flashcards (Chapter 18, p.301)

In Chapter 14, you can read through all of the USCIS civics questions and answers. Chapter 15 has these same questions asked as multiple choice questions to help you remember the correct answer.

Chapter 16 lets you practice with "questions only". Chapter 17 has the special 20 questions for qualified people who are at least 65 years old. Finally, in Chapter 18, the questions and answers are printed as flashcards that you can take out of this book and cut into paper cards for easy review and practice.

There is also an ebook with civics flashcards, *100 Question and Answer Flashcards for U.S. Citizenship Test Practice,* that go with this book and is availabile at most e-bookstores.

You can also listen to the civics questions and answers read online at *Welcome ESL* (**www.welcomeesl.com**).

"What happens after I finish the citizenship interview and English and civics tests?"

If you didn't pass.... The USCIS officer will tell you if you passed all of the sections. If there is anything that you didn't pass, you can come back on a different day and retake the parts that you missed.

If you pass.... The USCIS officer will tell you that you passed, congratulate you, and then you will sign papers. Later, you will attend a citizenship ceremony (usually on a different day) where you will repeat the Oath of Allegiance (reprinted in this book on page 102). Then you will officially be an American citizen.

 Review

The 4 Parts of the Naturalization Interview and How They Are Scored

Do you remember what the four parts of the citizenship interview are and how they are scored?

Try to list the four parts yourself first, then go to the next page to see if you were correct. The parts of the test can happen in any order during your interview, so any order that you list them in below is fine.

1._____

2. _____

3. _____

4._____

Check your answers on the next page.

Answers:

1. Interview questions in English. The USCIS officer decides if you can understand and speak basic English. Many questions about your life and work will come from the information on your N-400 form.

2. Reading English. The USCIS officer will show you 1-3 sentences. You must correctly read 1 of the sentences out loud.

3. Writing English. The USCIS officer will read 1-3 sentences to you. You must correctly write 1 sentence.

4. Civics. The USCIS officer will ask you 6-10 questions from the official list of 100 civics questions. You must answer 6 correctly.

Albert Einstein, receiving his certificate of American citizenship from Judge Phillip Forman

photo credit: Al Aumuller, New York World Telegram

6

Special Circumstances - Exemptions
When You Don't Have to Take All Parts of the Citizenship Test

Famous People in American History

Susan B. Anthony, Suffragette
(Worked for Women's Right to Vote)

Civics Test Question #77: What did Susan B. Anthony do?

Answer: She fought for women's rights

6

Special Circumstances and Exemptions

"Do I Have to Take All Parts of the Citizenship Test?"

The citizenship test has four parts. Usually, you will:

- answer questions about yourself and why you want to become a U.S. citizen;
- read a sentence in English
- write a sentence in English
- answer questions about U.S. civiics

Exemptions. Some people do **not** need to take all parts of the citizenship test. Some people do not need to know all the civics questions. Some people can take parts of the test in their native language, not English. Some people with disabilities may be able to bring someone with them to help.

This chapter explains the most common reasons that the citizenship test requirements can be changed for your own needs. You can see if USCIS makes any changes or additions to these requirements online at **www.uscis.gov.**

Exceptions, Exemptions, and Accommodations/Modifications (Changes)

Some people qualify for changes in their citizenship test requirements. These are called "exceptions", "exemptions" or "modifications". The reasons you can get an exception, exemption or modification are:

- disability
- age and/or
- length of time as a permanent resident.

English Language Exemptions

Some people do not have to take ("are exempt from") the English requirement (speaking, reading, writing English) because of their age and the number of years they have been a permanent resident. But they still must take the civics test.

If you are 50 years or Older....

If you are (1) 50 or older when you file for naturalization and (2) have lived as a permanent resident for 20 years, you do not need to take the English reading, writing, and speaking tests. This is called the "50/20" exception.

If you are 55 years or Older....

If you are (1) 55 or older when you file for naturalization and (2) have lived as a permanent resident in the US for 15 years, you do not need to take the English reading, writing and speaking tests. This is called the "55/15" exception.

If you qualify for the "50/20" or "55/15" exception, you can answer the citizenship interview questions in any language that you choose. You do not need to take the English tests. But you must take the civics test.

Interpreter/Translator.   If you have a waiver for age, you can bring someone with you to your interview to translate questions for you.

*Important Note: Tell the USCIS that you want a waiver BEFORE you are interviewed so they are prepared. Write this in the letter you send with your application. You can write "50/20" or "55/15" in large numbers on top of your N-400 application.

Civics Test Modifications

Take the Civics Test in Your Native Language

You may be allowed to take the civics test in your native language if:

- you have been a permanent resident for 20 years or more;
- and you do not understand English well enough to be tested orally in English.

Test on 20 Civics Questions Only ("65/20")

You only need to know 20 of the 100 civics questions IF:

- you have been a permanent resident for 20 years and
- you are 65 years old or older

This is called "65/20". ("65 years old + a permanent resident for 20 years").

"If I am 65 years old and qualify to study 20 civics questions only, what are the 20 questions I need to know?"

The 20 civics questions you need to know are chosen from the USCIS list of 100 civics questions. They are marked with an * on all the lists of civics questions in this book. They are also listed in a separate section, beginning on page 287.

If you take the test in your native language, you must bring an interpreter.

Important: If you take the civics test in your native language, you must bring an interpreter with you to your interview. This person can be anyone who is fluent in English and your native language.

Medical Disability Exceptions for English and Civics Tests

There are other ways to get an exception to the English and civics requirements. Some people have a physical or mental disability that makes these tests very difficult for them. If you have a medical disability you can ask for an exception.

Question: "What form do I need to request a medical exception?"

Answer: Form N-648 "Medical Certificate for Disablity Exceptions".

This certificate must be completed by a licensed doctor or licensed clinical psychologist.

Disability Accommodation

USCIS will make an accommodation or modification if you have a physical or mental problem that makes it impossible for you to complete the citizenship process. You should write what you need in from USCIS in the space in Section 3 of your N-400 form. You can also include it in your cover letter.

An example of a reason to request an accommodation would be if you have a disability that makes it difficult to take your Oath of Allegiance because you can't stand up for a long time or you need wheelchair access. There are many possible reasons for difficulties.

Disability Waiver

"Will USCIS make changes to the test for me if I have a disability?"

Yes, USCIS will help. Some examples, from USCIS: "For example, if you use a wheelchair, we will make sure you can be fingerprinted, interviewed, and sworn in at a location that is wheelchair accessible."

If you are hearing impaired, the officer conducting your interview will speak loudly and slowly.

If you need an American sign language interpreter at your interview or at the oath ceremony, please write that on your Form N-400 in the section that asks about disabilities so USCIS can have an ASL interpreter there for you.

If you use a service animal, like a guide dog, your animal may come with you to your interview and oath ceremony.

If you have a physical or mental disability that makes it impossible for you to learn English, USCIS may say that you do not need to take the English and civics tests.

"What should I do if I have a disability?"

If you cannot learn English because of a disability, you can take the interview and civics test in your native language. If your disability makes that impossible, tell USCIS. They may say that you do not need to take the tests.

A doctor must document a Disability Waiver Request

There are many different kinds of disabilities. The USCIS will change the test for you if a doctor feels that you have a physical or emotional reason that you cannot answer civics questions or cannot learn English.

If you cannot learn English, your doctor must complete the USCIS form N-648 and explain your disability and why you must be tested in your native language.

"How can I ask for this waiver?"

To request the disability waiver, you need two things.

(1) Your N-400 form, Part 3, Question H.

On the N-400, go to Part 3, Question H, and check "Yes". This tells the USCIS that you have a disability.

(2) Your doctor completes Form N-648.

Ask your doctor to complete Form N-648, "Medical Certification for Disability Exceptions".

He must explain: (1) **what** part of the citizenship test you cannot take and 2) **why** your disability makes it too difficult for you to take the citizenship interview and/or the civics and English language tests.

Mail forms N-400 and **N-648** to USCIS when you apply for citizenship. Remember to keep copies of any information from a doctor and anything you send to USCIS.

"How can I get the disability waiver form?"

You can get this form from the USCIS website: www.uscis.gov
Or call USCIS at: 800-870-3676.

Other Accommodations for Disabilities

If you have a disability, you may need help to get into the USCIS office. Or you may need help to take the test. Have your doctor write a letter about your disability. The doctor can recommend that your friend or family member goes with you to the USCIS testing office to help you.

"How will USCIS know that I need special help?"

Your N-400 Form. To tell the USCIS that you need help, look at your N-400 form.

In Part 3, question #1, you need to check "Yes". Then write the reason you need help and the kind of help that you need.

For example, you can write: "I use a wheelchair and cannot climb stairs." Or, "I take medicine that makes me very nervous and I need to bring my daughter to the interview to help me."

"Do I need a letter from my doctor about my disability?"

Yes. It is a good idea to include a letter from your doctor to USCIS. She should explain what your disability is and what accommodation (help) or modification (change) you need so that you can take your citizenship test.

Show the doctor this page and this chapter so she understands what you need. Give her your N-400 form so she can answer "Yes" in Part 3, Question #1 and then write the reason. She should write a short letter about your medical problem and what kind of help you need to take the test. Give her the N-648 form to complete, too.

Mail the doctor's letter to the USCIS in the same envelope with your N-400 form and ask the post office worker to send the envelope "certified mail, return receipt requested".

"The USCIS already has my N-400 form and they don't know about my disability. What should I do?"

After you receive your interview notice, have your doctor write a letter explaining what you will need and send it to the USCIS district office that will interview you. You can send the doctor's letter and the completed cover letter that follows page 62 of this book. This will make it easy for USCIS to identify you and understand the problem.

Continuous Residence Exception

Most exceptions are made because of age, permanent residency, or disability. But if you do some kinds of work overseas you may be eligible for an exception to the continuous residence requirement. For more information about this exception, check with your employer or the USCIS website: **www.uscis.gov.**

7

Websites and Other Helpful Resources

Famous People in American History

Abraham Lincoln
President during the Civil War

Civics Test Question #75: Name one important thing that Abraham Lincoln did?

Answer: He freed the slaves.

7

U.S. Government Websites and Other Helpful Resources

If you have a question for the U.S. government and don't know where to call, begin with 1-800-FED-INFO (or 1-800-333-4636) for more information.
If you are hard-of-hearing, call 1-800-326-2996.

USCIS

U.S. Citizenship and Immigration Services (USCIS)
Get USCIS forms, by calling 1-800-870-3676 or looking on the USCIS website at http://www.uscis.gov
Phone for customer service: 1-800-375-5283
For hearing impaired: 1-800-767-1833

U.S. Government Information

http://www.usa.gov/Contact.shtml
Go here to get questions answered from the U.S. government.

http://www.welcometousa.gov
This is a U.S. government website for new immigrants.

http://www.usa.gov
This is the U.S. government website for general information.

U.S. Government Information – in Spanish

http://www.usa.gov/gobiernousa/index.shtml

U.S. Government Departments

Department of Education (ED)

U.S. Department of Education
400 Maryland Avenue SW
Washington, DC 20202
Phone: 1-800-872-5327
For hearing impaired: 1-800-437-0833
http://www.ed.gov

Department of Health and Human Services (HHS)

U.S. Department of Health and Human Services
200 Independence Avenue SW
Washington, DC 20201
Phone: 1-877-696-6775
http://www.hhs.gov

Department of Homeland Security (DHS)

U.S. Department of Homeland Security
Washington, DC 20528
http://www.dhs.gov

Department of Housing and Urban Development (HUD)

U.S. Department of Housing and Urban Development
451 7th Street SW
Washington, DC 20410
Phone: 202-708-1112
For hearing impaired: 202-708-1455
http://www.hud.gov

Department of Justice (DOJ)

U.S. Department of Justice
950 Pennsylvania Avenue NW
Washington, DC 20530-0001
Phone: 202-514-2000
http://www.usdoj.gov

U.S. Government Departments

Department of State (DOS)
U.S. Department of State
2201 C Street NW
Washington, DC 20520
Phone: 202-647-4000
http://www.state.gov

Other U.S. Government Agencies

Equal Employment Opportunity Commission (EEOC)
U.S. Equal Employment Opportunity Commission
1801 L Street NW
Washington, DC 20507
Phone: 1-800-669-4000
For hearing impaired: 1-800-669-6820
http://www.eeoc.gov

Internal Revenue Service (IRS)
Phone: 1-800-829-1040
For hearing impaired: 1-800-829-4059
http://www.irs.gov

Selective Service System (SSS)
Registration Information Office
PO Box 94638
Palatine, IL 60094-4638
Phone: 847-688-6888
For hearing impaired: 847-688-2567
http://www.sss.gov

U.S. Customs and Border Protection (CBP)
Phone: 202-354-1000
http://www.cbp.gov

U.S. Immigration and Customs Enforcement (ICE)
http://www.ice.gov

Social Security Administration (SSA)
Office of Public Inquiries
6401 Security Boulevard
Baltimore, MD 21235
Phone: 1-800-772-1213
For hearing impaired: 1-800-325-0778
http://www.socialsecurity.gov or
http://www.segurosocial.gov/espanol/

Congress

www.senate.gov — You can find the names of your U.S. senator here.

www.house.gov — You can find the name of your U.S. representative here.

Visa information

http://www.travel.state.gov/ — Go here for visa information—and to check processing time by country—from the U.S. State Department.

U.S. Embassies and Consulates

http://www.usembassy.gov/ — Here is the information you need to contact U.S. consulates around the world.

You Can Also Go To....

Check: www.welcomeesl.com for new information and practice materials. It also has links to many other websites with English and citizenship information.

Libraries also have helpful information, including books, free CDs, DVDs., and free computers to use.

To Find a Citizenship Class or ESL Program Near You

Go to: `http://www.literacydirectory.org/` You can search there for a citizenship or English program in your area.

English Language Resources

`www.grammardesk.com` — This is an excellent resource for English learners and teachers.

`www.spellcity.com` — You can create your own spelling lists and practice with this self-correcting software.

For College Preparation (TOEFL)

`www.toefldesk.com` — This is a useful website if you want to go to college in the U.S. and are interested in preparing for TOEFL (Test of English as a Foreign Language).

Advice on Using the Internet to Translate from English into Other Languages

Google Translate
http://translate.google.com/

If you want to know how to pronounce a word or sentence, type it into **http://translate.google.com/** and click on the icon to hear the word or sentence in English.

Google translate does not always use perfect pronunciation, and it does not always translate sentences correctly. But the pronunciation can usually be understood by English speakers. And Google translations can be helpful when you see an unfamiliar word or sentence, to give you a better understanding of the meaning.

Google translate is not always correct, but if you practice using it for small words and phrases, it can help you with translations when you need to understand something in English and want to translate it into your own language. It is *not* a good idea to use online programs to translate from your own language into English. The results are usually difficult for native English speakers to understand and may even make mistakes that are embarrassing for you.

Google can be helpful with pronunciation, but a better idea is to learn to use the pronunciation guides in the English language dictionaries.

Babelfish (Yahoo)
http://babelfish.yahoo.com/

Babelfish is another site that helps you translate words and phrases. It is less accurate than Google, but may help you understand the meaning of English words when you have no other resources available.

8

"What Happens at the USCIS Citizenship Interview?"
Know What to Expect When You Talk with the USCIS Officer

Famous People in American History

Woodrow Wilson
28th President of the U.S.

Civics Test Question #80: Who was President during World War I?

Answer: (Woodrow) Wilson

8

"What Happens at the Citizenship Interview?"

"How many parts are there to the citizenship test?"

There are four (4) parts to your Citizenship Test:

1. The oral interview in English
2. reading English
3. writing English
4. the Civics Test

To review from Chapter 5, when you go to the citizenship interview, usually only one person will interview you for all 4 parts of it. But sometimes one person will ask the N-400 questions and a different person will ask questions about civics and English. This is also normal at some offices.

This interviewer represents USCIS and is called an "officer". The USCIS officer is employed by the U.S. government. She or he is not with the police or other law enforcement agencies.

The USCIS interviewer will have your application and all of your paperwork. She will ask questions about your N-400 application. This is your opportunity to show the interviewer that you are honest, will be a good citizen, and that you can understand and speak English.

Do not worry about your accent or grammar as long as you can be understood. Speak slowly if you need to. Ask the interviewer to repeat anything that you don't understand. You can say, "Could you please repeat that?" She will be glad to repeat a question for you, if you ask her.

The Day of Your Interview

__1. Be on time.

__2. Dress as if you are going to a job interview.

__3. Shake the interviewer's hand when you meet and say your full name (first name and last name).

__4. The interviewer will not try to trick you or surprise you. She will not mark you lower because you have an accent, but you need to be understood.

__5. If you do not understand something, it is good to say, "Could you please say that again?"

__6. Speak clearly and make eye contact. Look at the interviewer. Remember to smile.

__7. The interviewer will look at four things. Can you...

    (1) answer questions about your N-400 form;

    (2) read 1 of 3 simple sentences in English;

    (3) write 1 of 3 simple sentences in English;

    (4) answer 6 questions about the civics (history and geography) of the United States. These questions will always be chosen from the list of "100 Civics Questions". A special list of 20 questions for people who are over 65 years old and have been permanent residents for 20 years is also included in this book, in Chapter 17.

The USCIS officer will not ask you any surprise questions, or try to trick you. The USCIS interviewer cannot help you answer questions, but she wants you to be successful.

Next You Will Take the Civics, Reading, and Writing Tests

After you answer the interview questions, the officer will ask you to sign some documents. You will sign your 2 photographs. She will give you your N-400 Form and you will sign it. Then you will take the civics, reading and writing tests.

Civics: The USCIS officer will ask you 10 questions from the 100 official civics citizenship questions. They are listed in Chapter 14 which begins on page 225. When you get 6 of 10 questions right, she will stop.

> **Passing Score for Civics:** You must answer 6 civics questions correctly to pass.

Reading: Next, the officer will test your reading. She will show you a sentence in English and ask you to read it out loud. Take your time and read it to yourself silently first. You will read better orally if you have read it silently first. She will not ask you to explain what it means.

The officer can give you one, two or three (3) sentences to read. After you have read one (1) sentence correctly, she will stop and not ask you to read more.

> **Passing Score for Reading:** Read 1 sentence correctly.

Writing: Finally, the officer will test your writing. (Printing or hand-writing is fine). She will read a sentence to you in English and you will write it down. Your sentence does not have to be perfect, but the meaning should be clear. If you miss the sentence, don't worry. The officer can read you three sentences. You only need to write 1 sentence correctly.

> **Passing Score for Writing:** Write 1 sentence correctly.

After Your Interview

"If I don't pass, can I take it again?"

Yes. Most people pass the first time. But if you don't, you can retake the part you missed on a different day.

How to Retake the Test

If You Don't Pass

You can take the test twice. If you do not pass you will have one more opportunity to take the English and civics tests and to answer questions about yourself and your reasons for becoming a citizen.

If you pass some parts of the test at your first interview, you will be retested between 60 and 90 days from the date of your first interview, but you will be asked different questions. You will only be re-tested on the parts you didn't pass. USCIS will tell you when your application is approved and when you can retake the parts you missed.

If you do not pass the second time you are tested, you need to reapply again and pay again.

"I Passed! What happens next?"

Congratulations! Most people will pass their citizenship test on their first try. When you pass, you will become a U.S. citizen. The USCIS officer will ask you to sign some papers. USCIS will mail you a letter that will tell you the time and place for your citizenship ceremony.

At this ceremony, which may be in a small group or with hundreds of other people, you will say an *Oath of Allegiance*. Don't memorize it. The USCIS official will read it to the group and you will repeat it. The lines have been separated on page 102 to make the meaning clearer.

The *Pledge of Allegiance* or *Oath of Allegiance*?

"Allegiance" means "loyalty". *The Oath of Allegiance* (page 102) is said by new citizens at the citizenship ceremony to show their loyalty to their new country.

The *Oath of Allegiance* is not the same as the *Pledge of Allegiance* (below). The *Pledge of Allegiance* is what Americans say at certain events. They always stand when they say it, put their hand on their heart, and look at the American flag. The *Pledge of Allegiance* is said often, especially in schools, government meetings and sometimes before sports events.

Most Americans have never seen the *Oath of Allegiance*, but they learn the *Pledge of Allegiance* in elementary school. It is good for you to memorize this.

The Pledge of Allegiance

I pledge allegiance to the flag of the United States of America, and to the republic for which it stands, one nation, under God, with liberty and justice for all.

Unlike the Pledge of Allegiance, the Oath of Allegiance is only said at citizenship ceremonies. Most Americans have never heard it. You do not need to memorize it, but it is good to read and understand it. It is the final step in your citizenship process.

Oath of Allegiance

"I hereby declare, on oath, that I absolutely and entirely renounce and abjure all allegiance and fidelity to any foreign prince, potentate, state, or sovereignty, of whom or which I have heretofore been a subject or citizen;

that I will support and defend the Constitution and laws of the United States of America against all enemies, foreign and domestic;

that I will bear true faith and allegiance to the same;

that I will bear arms on behalf of the United States when required by the law;

that I will perform noncombatant service in the Armed Forces of the United States when required by the law;

that I will perform work of national importance under civilian direction when required by the law;

and that I take this obligation freely, without any mental reservation or purpose of evasion, so help me God."

"What Does the Oath of Allegiance Mean?"

Paragraph 1 is a promise that you will be loyal to the United States and not to any other country or leadership.

Paragraph 2 is your promise to support the Constitution and the other laws of the United States.

Paragraph 3 repeats your commitment to the Constitution and the U.S..

Paragraph 4 is a promise to carry a gun for the U.S. ("bear arms") if the law requires you to;

Paragraph 5 is a promise to serve in the U.S. military if the law requires you to;

Paragraph 6 is a promise to do work for the country if the law requires you to

Paragraph 7 is your statement that you have made this citizenship choice freely and agree to this promise completely.

After you have said the Oath of Allegiance, you are now officially a U.S. citizen.

9

Speaking English at Your Interview: Know Your N-400 Form

Famous People in American History

Franklin Roosevelt
32nd President of the United States

Civics Test Question #80: Who was President during the Great Depression and World War II?

Answer: (Franklin) Roosevelt

9

Speaking English at Your Interview
Know Your N-400 Form

The N-400 Form

The information you wrote on your N-400 citizenship application form is very important. The USCIS interviewer can ask you questions about anything on the N-400 form. You should know this information well and answer all questions honestly.

If you have any problems that could prevent you from becoming a U.S. citizen, you can explain the problem at your citizenship interview.

Your answers to questions about your N-400 form are very important to USCIS, and this chapter gives you practice answering questions about yourself. The following section has practice questions about different sections of your N-400 form. To get a blank copy of the form you can go online to **www.uscis.gov** or call the USCIS office at 1-800-870-3676.

You can also go to **www.welcomeesl.com** and follow the link to **www.uscis.gov**. Then download and print the form yourself. You can also watch the video of the USCIS sample interview at:

www.welcomeesl.com or **www.uscis.gov**

Citizenship Test Checklist - Review

Questions To Expect At Your Citizenship Test

Use this checklist to review and check (x) the parts of the interview you are prepared for. Then you will see the parts that are not checked. Those are the things you need to do.

I'm ready to:

___ Answer questions about any information on my *N-400* application form;

___ Correctly answer any 6 Civics Questions from the official U.S. government list;

___ Correctly read 1 of 3 sentences in English out loud;

___ Correctly write 1 of 3 sentences that the examiner (officer) will dictate to me to write down.

Special Note: If you are 65 years or older....
****

If you are 65 or older and have been a legal permanent resident of the United States for 20 or more years, you only need to know the civics questions that have been marked with an asterisk.* The complete list of these 20 questions begins on page 287.

You can also choose to take the civics test in any language you want and to have an interpreter/translator with you at the interview.

Unless you have a waiver, you must still take the English reading, and writing tests and show the officer that you can speak English.

What Countries Have You Been To?

The USCIS wants to know every date that you have left the United States during the time you were a permanent resident, especially in the last 5 years. Here is a worksheet where you can list this information. You will need it for your N-400 form.

Date You Left (Month/Day/Year)	Date You Came Back	Number of Days	Countries You Visited
For example: 3/25/2009	4/17/2009	24	Spain, England Morocco

"How Many Sections are on the N-400 Form?"

The USCIS interviewer will ask you many questions about the information on your citizenship application form (N-400 form).

There are two reasons you will be asked about the N-400 form: (1) to see that the information you wrote is truthful, and (2) so the USCIS officer can see that you understand and can speak English. (He will not score you lower because of an accent, as long as he can understand you.)

Your N-400 form has 10 sections of questions:

Part 1. Name

Part 2. Eligibility

Part 3. Information About You (e.g. social security number)

Part 4. Address and Phone Number

Part 5. Criminal Records Search Information (The INS examiner will probably not ask you about this).

Part 6. Residence and Employment

Part 7. Time Outside the U.S.

Part 8. Marital (Marriage) Information

Part 9. Your Children

Part 10. Other Questions

"How Does The Interview Begin?"

On the day of your appointment, arrive at least 15 minutes early. You will walk through a check-in area. Tell the security officer that you have a naturalization interview. He will ask to see your naturalization appointment letter and your I.D. Then you will go to the customer service waiting area until your name is called.

Your Interview Begins

A USCIS officer (interviewer) will come to the waiting area and call your name. Remember to smile at her (or him) and shake hands.

You will go into an office. You will not sit down yet. The officer will ask you to raise your right hand and swear an oath. She will ask you, "Do you solemnly swear to tell the truth, the whole truth and nothing but the truth, so help you God?"

You will answer, "I do," and then she will ask you to sit down.

Most of your citizenship interview will be about your answers on the N-400 application form. The officer will ask you questions about your application and decide if you have answered honestly and if you can speak and understand basic English.

If you don't understand something, it is good to ask the officer, "Could you please say that again?" or say, "I don't understand. Could you ask me that question in a different way?" When you ask these questions you are showing that you can use English. The officer will repeat any question if you ask her.

Citizenship Interview: An Example

Practice this interview. Have friends and relatives ask you the interview questions. You can see a complete example of a USCIS video interview online (in Spanish and English) at:

www.welcomeesl.com

You can also look for the video directly at **www.uscis.gov**

Q: **What is your name?**

A: Linda Smith

Q: **Have you ever used any other name?**

A: No.

Q: **Do you want to change your name?**

A: No, I don't.

Q: **What is your date of birth? (or "When were you born?")**

A: November 8, 1970

Q: **Where were you born?**

A: I was born in Paris, France.

Q: **Are you a citizen of France?**

A: Yes, I am.

Q: **Are either of your parents U.S. citizens?**

A: No, they are not citizens.

Q: Are you currently single, married, divorced or widowed?

    A: I am single.

Q: Where are you currently living?

    A: I live at 702 West First Street, in Los Angeles.

Q: Where are you working?

    A: I work at the county library.

Q: When was your last trip outside the U.S.

    A: About 4 months ago, I went to France to see my family. I was there for 2 weeks.

Q: Do you remember the day you returned to the United States?

    A: May 23.

****

The USCIS officer can ask you to give more information about any of your answers or anything you wrote on your application. Be prepared to answer questions about....

- Any **trips** you took outside of the U.S.;

- Any **marriages or divorces** you have had;

- Membership in any **controversial organizations**;

- If you ever were tried in court for a **crime** (bring papers of the court decision, if you have them);

- **U.S. military service** (If you are a man between 18 and 25, you need to show you registered for selective service);

- Your allegiance (loyalty) to the United States.

Practice Your Interview Answers

Here is a practice citizenship interview with Roberto Pablo Martin, a man from Mexico. Read his answers. Then practice your own answers to these questions. There is a lot of information on the N-400 form. These are some examples of the questions you can be asked from different parts of the form

It is good to write your own answer on the line below the answer that is given as an example. Then practice your interview with a friend. Your friend can ask the questions and you answer. Then you can ask the questions and the friend can answer. You need to hear how a citizenship interview sounds.

Part 1 – 4 (from N-400 form). Your Name and Other Identifying Information about You.

1. **What is your name? (or "Please state your full name")**

   My name is Roberto Pablo Martin.

Now write your own name in the space below. Then read the other questions and write your own answers on the line.

My name is _____

2. **Is Martin your family name? (or, another way to ask this question is, "Is Martin your last name?")**

   Yes, Martin is my last name.

Your answer:

Yes, _____

114

3. How do you spell that?

M-a-r-t-i-n

Your answer:

_____

4. What name is on your Green Card (Permanent Resident Visa)?

Roberto Martin

(Or say, "The name on my Green Card is Roberto Martin.")

Your answer:

_____

5. Is "Pablo" your middle name?

Yes. Pablo is my middle name.

Your answer:

_____

_____

6. Have you used any other legal name?

No. I have never used another legal name.

(Or, "Yes, I have used the name 'Robert Martin' at work.")

Your answer:

_____

7. Some people change their name when they become a citizen. Do you want to change your name?

No, I don't want to change my name. (Or "Yes. I want to change my name to Robert Martin.")

Your answer:

_____

8. To become a U.S. citizen, you have to be a legal Permanent Resident for at least 5 years. When did you become a Permanent Resident?

I became a Permanent Resident in 2004.

Your answer:

_____

9. Are you eligible for citizenship because your spouse (husband or wife) is a citizen?

Yes. My wife/husband is a citizen. (Or, if your spouse is not a citizen, go to answer Question 12).

Your answer:

Yes, _____

_____

_____

10. When did she become a citizen? (Or, if it is your husband, "When did he become a citizen?")

She became a citizen in 2008. Or "She was born in the United States."

_____

_____

11. Do you live together?

Yes, we do.

(Note: If you are married to a U.S. citizen, be prepared to answer questions about your life together. Remember to always remain polite and calm. The INS interviewer wants to know that your marriage and relationship are real and were not done just to help you become a citizen. It is the USCIS officer's job to decide if your answers are true.)

Use the space below for any details you might want to remember—your spouse's birthday, the year you were married, and so on. You may be asked questions about your children and your life together. These are normal citizenship questions that the USCIS will ask if you married a U.S. citizen or permanent resident.

_____

_____

_____

_____

12. If your wife (husband) is not a U.S. citizen, what country is she from? What is her immigration status?

She is from Canada. She has a permanent resident visa.

_____

_____

13. What is your birth date?

I was born June 3, 1980.

_____

_____

14. What is your Social Security Number?

My Social Security number is 006-02-5514.

_____

_____

15. What is your country of origin? (Where are you from?)

I am from Mexico.

_____

16. **Where do you live now?**

I live in Los Angeles.

_____

17. **What is your current address? (Editor's note: You live "at" an address, "on" a street, "in" an apartment, city, state or country.)**

I live at 526 First St., Apartment 51, in Los Angeles.

_____

_____

18. **What is your phone number?**

My phone number is (555) 825-4777.

_____

_____

19. **What city do you live in?**

I live in Los Angeles.

_____

20. What state is that in?

Los Angeles is in California. (Or say, "California").

_____

_____

21. What is your zip code?

My zip code is 91307.

_____

Part 5. Checking for a Criminal Past

The INS needs information about your fingerprints, weight and height to check for a past criminal record. Fill in this information (if any) before you mail in your form. They will not ask about this during your interview.

Part 6. Employment and Residence
(Where You Work and Live)

22. Where do you work?

I work at the Regent Hotel.

_____

23. What do you do there? (or "What is your job?")

I'm a waiter.

---

24. Have you worked at any other jobs in the last 5 years?

Yes. I worked at Pacific Restaurant. I was a cook.

---

25. Have you ever left the United States since you became a Permanent Resident?

Yes. I went to Mexico in May, 2009.

---

26. How long were you there?

I was there for two months.

Part 7. Time Outside the U.S.

What Countries Have You Been To?

The USCIS wants to know every date that you have left the United States during the time you were a permanent resident, especially in the last 5 years. Here is the worksheet where you can list this information. (There is also a worksheet on page 109).

Date You Left (Month/Day/Year)	Date You Came Back	Number of Days	Countries You Visited
For example: 3/25/2009	4/17/2009	24	Spain, England Morocco

Part 8. Marital (Marriage) Information

The USCIS officer wants to be sure that you did not marry your spouse just to become a U.S. citizen. If you married an American citizen, you may be asked if you have joint bank accounts, if you know your spouse's best friend's name, and questions about your house or apartment.

You may be asked other personal questions so USCIS can understand that your marriage is real. There may be one or two questions like this, or more. Don't feel offended by anything that you are asked. It is the officer's job to be sure that no one is approved for citizenship due to a fraudulent marriage.

1. What is your spouse's name?

_____

2. When was your husband or wife born?

_____

3. Where was your husband or wife born?

_____

4. How did you meet your husband or wife?

_____

5. When and where were you married?

_____

6. Where does your spouse work?

_____

7. Do you have a joint bank account? Where do you bank?

_____

8. Are both of your names on your mortgage or apartment rental agreement?

_____

9. Have either of you been married before?

_____

10. Have either of you been widowed or divorced?

_____

List any other important personal information that might be helpful for the USCIS officer to know about your marriage and life together:

_____

_____

_____

_____

_____

_____

_____

_____

_____

Part 9. Your Children
Children and Grandchildren Information

USCIS will probably not ask for information about your children unless they want to be sure that the marriage is real and not fraudulent. If you are married to an American citizen, USCIS may ask for these kinds of details to be sure your marriage is not just for the purpose of getting citizenship. Use your judgment if it is worth your time to complete this information. (USCIS will probably not ask for it.)

List each person's: Name – place of birth – birthdate – age – school – grade level.

1,_____

_____

_____

_____

2._____

_____

_____

_____

_____

_____

_____

_____

_____

_____

_____

_____

Family Information and Other Notes

Family Information and Other Notes

Part 10. Additional Questions
Explaining any problems

The questions for this section are all about possible problems. These are problems that USCIS needs to know about. If you answer, "Yes", to any of these, you should include a written explanation when you send in your N-400 form.

A written explanation should:

(1) explain why your answer was "Yes", and

(2) give any information that helps to explain your answer. The interviewer will ask you about any "Yes" answer. You should remember your written answer and be able to explain the problem when the USCIS interviewer asks you about it.

The questions in Part 10 show problems that might prevent citizenship. The interviewer will give you the opportunity to explain any problems. You can use the questions below to practice doing this.

There is space after each question in the following pages for you to write down a good, honest explanation for any problems. If you have any documents that will help the USCIS officer understand the situation, bring the documents with you to the interview.

Prepare for difficult questions before you go to the interview. Be prepared to talk calmly about any problems.

Part 10. Explain Any Problems

If you answered "Yes" to any of these questions on your N-400 form, be prepared to explain the problem.

1. Have you ever claimed to be a U.S. citizen (in writing or any other way)?

_____

_____

2. Have you ever registered to vote in any Federal, State, or local election in the United States?

_____

_____

3. Have you ever voted in any Federal, State, or local election in the United States?

_____

_____

4. Since becoming a lawful permanent resident, have you ever failed to file a required Federal, State, or local tax return?

_____

_____

5. Do you owe any Federal, State, or local taxes that are overdue?

_____

_____

6. Do you have any title of nobility in any foreign country?

_____

_____

7. Have you ever been declared legally incompetent or been confined to a mental institution within the last five years?

_____

_____

B. Affiliations

8. a. Have you ever been a member of or associated with any organization, association, fund foundation, party, club, society, or similar group in the United States or in any other place?

_____

_____

b. If you answered "Yes" to 8a, know the name of each group, party or organization.

_____

_____

_____

_____

9. Have you ever been a member of or in any way associated *(either directly or indirectly)* with:

a. The Communist Party?
b. Any other totalitarian party?
c. A terrorist organization?

_____

_____

10. Have you ever advocated *(either directly or indirectly)* the overthrow of any government by force or violence?

_____

11. Have you ever persecuted *(either directly or indirectly)* any person because of race, religion, national origin, membership in a particular social group, or political opinion?

_____

12. Between March 23, 1933, and May 8, 1945, did you work for or associate in any way *(either directly or indirectly)* with:

a. The Nazi government of Germany?

_____

_____

b. Any government in any area (1) occupied by, (2) allied with, or (3) established with the help of the Nazi government of Germany?

_____

_____

c. Any German, Nazi, or S.S. military unit, paramilitary unit, self-defense unit, vigilante unit, citizen unit, police unit, government agency or office, extermination camp, concentration camp, prisoner of war camp, prison, labor camp, or transit camp?

_____

_____

_____

_____

_____

C. Continuous Residence

If you answer "Yes" to any of the questions below, it is a problem that USCIS can ask you about. Write any explanation that will help you on the lines below any question that you answer, "Yes".

Since becoming a lawful permanent resident of the United States:

13. Have you ever called yourself a "nonresident" on a Federal, State, or local tax return?

_____

_____

14. Have you ever failed to file a Federal, State, or local tax return because you considered yourself to be a "nonresident"?

_____

_____

_____

_____

_____

_____

_____

D. Good Moral Character

For the purposes of this application, you must answer "Yes" to the following questions, if they are true, even if your records were sealed or otherwise cleared or if anyone, including a judge, law enforcement officer, or attorney, told you that you no longer have a record.

15. Have you ever committed a crime or offense for which you were not arrested?

_____

_____

16. Have you ever been arrested, cited, or detained by any law enforcement officer (including USCIS or former INS and military officers) for any reason?

_____

_____

17. Have you ever been charged with committing any crime or offense?

_____

_____

_____

_____

18. Have you ever been convicted of a crime or offense?

_____

_____

19. Have you ever been placed in an alternative sentencing or a rehabilitative program (for example: diversion, deferred prosecution, withheld adjudication, deferred adjudication)?

_____

_____

_____

_____

20. Have you ever received a suspended sentence, been placed on probation, or been paroled?

_____

_____

_____

_____

_____

_____

21. Have you ever been in jail or prison?

_____

_____

_____

_____

Questions 22 through 33

If you answer "Yes" to any of these questions, you should send with your application:

(1) your written explanation why your answer was "Yes". and

(2) any additional information or documentation that helped explain your answer.

If asked, be sure to explain to the USCIS interviewer:

(1) Why were you arrested, cited, detained, or charged?

_____

_____

_____

_____

_____

_____

(2) The date you were arrested, cited, detained, or charged. (mm/dd/yyyy. For example, May 15, 1996 would be written: 05/15/1996. Remember that Americans always write the date with the month first).

_____

_____

(3) Where were you arrested, cited, detained, or charged? (City, State, Country)

_____

_____

(4) Outcome or disposition of the arrest, citation, detention, or charge (Some possible answers are: *"No charges were filed", "The charges were dismissed", "I served jail time", "I received probation", etc.*)

_____

_____

_____

_____

_____

_____

22. Have you ever:

a. Been a habitual drunkard?

_____

_____

b. Been a prostitute, or procured anyone for prostitution?

_____

_____

c. Failed to support your dependents or to pay alimony?

_____

_____

_____

d. Sold or smuggled controlled substances, illegal drugs, or narcotics?

_____

_____

_____

e. Been married to more than one person at the same time?

_____

_____

f. Helped anyone enter or try to enter the United States illegally?

_____

_____

_____

g. Gambled illegally or received income from illegal gambling?

_____

_____

23. Have you ever given false or misleading information to any U.S. government official while applying for immigration benefits or to prevent deportation, exclusion, or removal?

_____

_____

_____

_____

24. Have you ever lied to any U.S. Government official to gain entry or admission into the United States?

_____

_____

E. Removal, Exclusion, and Deportation Proceedings

25. Are removal, exclusion, rescission, or deportation proceedings pending against you?

_____

_____

26. Have you ever been removed, excluded, or deported from the United States?

_____

_____

27. Have you ever *been ordered* to be removed, excluded or deported from the United States?

_____

_____

_____

_____

28. Have you ever applied for any kind of relief from removal, exclusion, or deportation?

_____

_____

F. Military Service

29. Have you ever served in the U.S. Armed Forces?

_____

_____

30. Have you ever left the United States to avoid being drafted into the U.S. Armed Forces?

_____

_____

31. Have you ever applied for any kind of exemption from military service in the U.S. Armed Forces?

_____

_____

_____

32. Have you ever deserted from the U.S. Armed Forces?

_____

_____

G. Selective Service Registration

33. Are you a male who lived in the United States at any time between your 18th and 26th birthdays in any status except as a lawful nonimmigrant?

_____

_____

If you answered "YES," but you did not register with the Selective Service System and are still under 26 years old, you must register before you apply for citizenship (naturalization).

_____

_____

If you answered "YES," but you did not register with the Selective Service and you are now 26 years old or older, attach a statement explaining why you did not register.

_____

_____

_____

H. Oath Requirements

If you answer "No" to any of the next questions, 34 to 39, be sure to know your written explanation on the N-400 Form and be able to explain your answer to the USCIS interviewer. (The Oath of Allegiance is on page 102.)

34. Do you support the Constitution and the form of government of the United States?

_____

_____

_____

_____

35. Do you understand the full Oath of Allegiance to the United States?

_____

_____

36. Are you willing to take the full Oath of Allegiance to the United States?

_____

_____

_____

_____

37. If the law requires it, are you willing to bear arms on behalf of the United States?

_____

38. If the law requires it, are you willing to perform noncombatant services in the U.S. Armed Forces?

_____

_____

39. If the law requires it, are you willing to perform work of national importance under civilian direction?

_____

_____

My Notes

If you want to write any reminders or notes for yourself about interview questions that you want to remember, write them here:

_____

_____

_____

_____

_____

10

Reading Test Practice

Famous People in American History

Dwight Eisenhower
34th President of the United States

Civics Test Question #82: Before he was President, Eisenhower was a general. What war was he in?

Answer: World War II

10

Reading Test Practice

Reading Vocabulary List (USCIS Recommended)

Your reading test will be 1-3 sentences. You must read one (1) of three (3) sentences correctly to show that you can read English. This chapter lists the words the USCIS recommends for you to know, but other words may be tested.

Practice reading the words in this section out loud.

To hear these words correctly pronounced, listen to the audio file at **www.welcomeesl.com.** Then practice reading the sentences on page 150. You should also practice reading the sentences in Chapter 13 which begins on page 213.

USCIS Recommended Reading Vocabulary

Question Words

how
what
when
where
why
who

Other

a
for *
here *
in *
of *
on *
the*
to *
we *

Verbs

can *
come
do/does
elects
have/has*
be/is/are/was *
lives/lived *
meet
name
pay *
vote *
want *

Other (content)

colors
dollar bill *
first *
largest *
many
most *
north *
one *
people *
second *
south *

People

George Washington
Abraham Lincoln

Places

United States   U.S.
America

USCIS Recommended Reading Vocabulary (cont.)

Civics

American flag
Bill of Rights
capital *
citizens *
city
Congress *
country
Father of Our Country *
government
President *
right *
Senators *
state/states *
White House

Holidays

Presidents' Day
Memorial Day
Flag Day
Independence Day
Labor Day
Columbus Day
Thanksgiving

A Tip!

Read and listen to English as much as you can. The more you read English—including close captioned television programs or English language subtitles—the more words you will know and remember.

Reading Practice: The USCIS does not publish the sentences they use. But here are a few examples that you can practice. There are more practice sentences on page 214.

Important: Read out loud, and speak clearly. (1) Show that you can read all the words in the sentence. (2) Sound like you understand the words; and (3) do not pause too long. You can listen to these sentences at:

www.welcomeesl.com

1. People vote to elect the President.
2. There are 100 Senators in Congress.
3. The White House is in Washington, D.C..
4. George Washington was the Father of Our Country.

A.

Read the words below. Then choose the best word to complete each of the sentences. Remember to capitalize the first word of each sentence.

what	**where**	**who**	**the**	**to**	**on**	**in**	**at**

1. _____ is the highest law of the country?

2. _____ do you live?

3. _____ lives in the White House?

4. I live _____ 142 First Avenue.

5. I live _____ Fairfield Street, _____ New York.

6. I go _____ school every day.

Now try these:

B.

south	Congress	most	many	largest
	the	senators	capital	

1. Washington, D.C. is the nation's_____.

2. _____ different people live in _____ United States.

3. Alaska is the _____ state.

4. Mexico is _____ of the United States.

5. _____ makes the laws.

6. _____ Americans know the Pledge of Allegiance.

Answers:

A (page 150): 1. What 2. Where 3 Who 4. at
5. on, in 6. to

B (page 151): 1. capital 2. Many*, the 3. largest
4. south 5. Congress 6. Most*

*Always read through all the choices and choose the best answer. You can see that "many" would be correct in #2 or #6. But you should only put it as the answer for #2 because "most" is correct for #6 but incorrect for #2.

11

Writing Test Practice

Practice tip: Have someone read you sentences with these vocabulary words. Practice writing down sentences as they are dictated (spoken) to you.

Famous People in American History

Martin Luther King, Jr.
Civil Rights Leader

Civics Test Question #85: What did Martin Luther King, Jr. do?

Answer: He fought for civil rights.

11

Writing Test Practice

The USCIS officer will read 1-3 short sentences and ask you to write them. (You can choose to print or handwrite.) You must only write one (1) out of the three (3) sentences correctly.

The USCIS does not tell the words that they use for this test. But they have a list of words they recommend for reading (see the list on page 148) and writing. You can practice writing the recommended USCIS words in this chapter. You can also have a friend read the list to you and test yourself by writing the words you hear on a piece of paper. Then use the blank lines in this chapter to practice writing anything that you missed.

Many of these words are also on the USCIS Reading List on page 148. Words that are on both lists are marked with an * and are listed separately for you in this chapter on page 161.

The sentences the USCIS officer dictates will be simple. Remember to capitalize names, dates, titles, and the first letter of the sentence. Remember to put a period at the end of a sentence. Put a question mark at the end of a question. For example, how would you fix the following sentence? Write it correctly on the lines below.

the white house is the home of president obama in washington dc

_____

_____

Corrected sentence:
The White House is the home of President Obama in Washington, D.C..

Writing Vocabulary List (USCIS Recommended)

February   _____

September _____

May   _____

October   _____

June   _____

November   _____

July   _____

Civics

American Indian _____

capital   _____

citizens   _____

Civil War   _____

Congress   _____

Father of Our Country _____

_____

flag _____

free _____

freedom of speech _____

_____

President   _____

right   _____

People

Adams   _____

Lincoln   _____

Washington _____

Senators   _____

state   _____

states   _____

White House _____

Verbs

be _____

is _____

was _____

can _____

come _____

elect _____

have _____

has _____

live _____

lived _____

meets_____

pay _____

vote _____

want *_____

Holidays

Presidents Day _____

Columbus Day _____

Thanksgiving _____

Flag Day _____

Labor Day _____

Memorial Day_____

Independence Day _____

Places

Alaska _____

California _____

Canada _____

Delaware _____

Mexico _____

New York City _____

Washington, D.C. _____

United States _____

Other

and _____

be _____

blue _____

dollar bill * _____

during _____

fifty / 50 _____

first * _____

for * _____

here * _____

in * _____

largest * _____

most * _____

north * _____

of * _____

on * _____

one hundred (100) _____

people _____

red _____

second* _____

south* _____

taxes _____

the * _____

to * _____

we * _____

white_____

A Tip!

Remember: How to Write a Sentence Correctly

Question: What does every sentence begin with?

Answer: Every sentence begins with a **capital letter**.
Remember to put a capital letter at the beginning of a sentence.

Question: What does every sentence end with?

Answer: Every sentence ends with a **period**. Remember to put a period at the end of a sentence and a question mark at the end of a question.

If you do not get the first or second sentence correct, the officer will read a third sentence to you. You must write one of the three sentences correctly to pass this section.

Words That are on Both USCIS Lists

Here are the words that are the same on the USCIS Reading Vocabulary and Writing Vocabulary Lists.

can _____

capital_____

citizen _____

citizens _____

Congress _____

dollar bill _____

Father of Our Country _____

first _____

for _____

has _____

have _____

here _____

in _____

is _____

largest _____

lived _____

lives _____

most_____

north _____

of_____

on _____

one _____

pay _____

people _____

President _____

right _____

second_____

Senators _____

south_____

state _____

states _____

the _____

to _____

vote _____

want _____

was _____

we _____

12

Vocabulary for Reading and Writing Practice
500 of the Most Common Words in English

Famous People in American History

Barack Obama
44th President of the United States

Civics Test Question #28: Who is the President of the United States now?

Answer: (Barack) Obama

12

Vocabulary for Reading and Writing
500 of the Words Most Often Used in English

The USCIS does not tell which words it uses for reading and writing sentences. To prepare for these tests, it is helpful to practice the USCIS recommended vocabulary. It is also a good idea to know the 500 most commonly used words in English, which are all included in this chapter, in order of frequency.

Recommended Practice Schedule: Regular daily practice—even if it is only ten or fifteen minutes—is better than practicing for a long time, but not very often. Short, frequent practices will help you remember.

The words below have been grouped into 19 words per week (20 for Week 1), but choose the practice schedule that works best for you. Look up any words you don't know in the dictionary. The dictionary will give you the correct pronunciation, the definition and an example of the word used in a sentence.

Week 1: 1 - 20

1. the _____

2. and _____

3. a _____

4. of _____

5. to _____

6. is _____

7. in _____

8. you _____

9. that _____

10. it _____

11. he _____

12. was _____

13. are _____

14. for _____

15. on _____

16. as _____

17. with _____

18. I _____

19. his _____

20. they _____

Week 2: 21 - 40

21. be_____

22. at _____

23. this _____

24. have _____

25. from_____

26. or _____

27. one _____

28. had _____

29. by _____

30. word _____

31. but _____

32. what _____

33. not _____

34. all _____

35. were _____

36. we _____

37. when _____

38. your _____

39. can _____

40. said _____

Week 3: 41 - 60

41. there _____

42. use _____

43. an _____

44. each _____

45. which _____

46. she _____

47. do _____

48. how _____

49. their _____

50. if _____

51. will _____

52. up _____

53. other _____

54. about _____

55. out _____

56. many _____

57. them _____

58. then _____

59. these _____

60. so _____

Week 4: 61 - 80

61. some _____

62. her _____

63. would _____

64. make _____

65. like _____

66. him _____

67. into _____

68. time _____

69. has _____

70. look _____

71. two _____

72. more _____

73. write _____

74. go _____

75. see _____

76. number _____

77. no _____

78. could _____'

79. way _____

80. people _____

Week 5: 81-100

81. my _____

82. than _____

83. first _____

84. water_____

85. been _____

86. call _____

87. who _____

88. its _____

89. oil_____

90. now _____

91. find _____

92. long_____

93. down_____

94. day_____

95. did _____

96. get _____

97. come_____

98. made_____

99. may_____

100. part _____

Week 6: 101 - 120

101. over _____

102. new _____

103. sound _____

104. take _____

105. only _____

106. little _____

107. work _____

108. know _____

109. place_____

110. year _____

111. live _____

112. me_____

113. give_____

114. back _____

115. most _____

116. very _____

117. after_____

118. our _____

119. thing _____

120. just _____

Week 7: 121 - 140

121. name _____

122. good _____

123. man _____

124. sentence _____

125. think _____

126. say _____

127. great _____

128. before _____

129. much _____

130. mean _____

131. old _____

132. boy _____

133. follow_____

134. around _____

135. also _____

136. where _____

137. help _____

138. through _____

139. line _____

140. right _____

Week 8: 141 - 160

141. too _____

142. any _____

143. same _____

144. tell _____

145. came _____

146. want_____

147. show_____

148. form_____

149. three _____

150. small_____

151. set _____

152. put _____

153. end_____

154. does _____

155. another_____

156. well _____

157. large _____

158. must _____

159. big _____

160. even _____

Week 9: 161 - 180

161. such _____

162. because_____

163. turn _____

164. here _____

165. why _____

166. ask _____

167. went _____

168. men _____

169. need _____

170. read _____

171. land _____

172. different _____

173. home_____

174. us _____

175. move _____

176. try _____

177. kind _____

178. hand _____

179. picture _____

180. again _____

Week 10: 181 - 200

181. change _____

182. off _____

183. play _____

184. spell _____

185. air _____

186. away _____

187. animal _____

188. house _____

189. point _____

190. page _____

191. letter _____

192. mother _____

193. answer _____

194. found _____

195. study _____

196. still _____

197. learn _____

198. should _____

199. American _____

200. world _____

Week 11: 201 - 220

201. high _____

202. every _____

203. near_____

204. food _____

205. add _____

206. between_____

207. own _____

208. below_____

209. country _____

210. plant _____

211. last _____

212. school _____

213. father_____

214. keep _____

215. tree _____

216. never_____

217. start _____

218. city _____

219. earth _____

220. eye _____

Week 12: 221 - 240

221. light _____

222. thought_____

223. head _____

224. under _____

225. story _____

226. saw _____

227. left _____

228. don't _____

229. few _____

230. while _____

231. along _____

232. might _____

233. close_____

234. something _____

235. seem_____

236. next _____

237. hard _____

238. open _____

239. example_____

240 begin_____

Week 13: 241 - 260

241. life_____

242. always _____

243. those _____

244. both_____

245. paper _____

246. together_____

247. got _____

248. group _____

249. often _____

250. run _____

251. important _____

252. until _____

253. children _____

254. side _____

255. feet _____

256. car _____

257. mile _____

258. night _____

259. walk _____

260. white _____

Week 14: 261 - 280

261. sea _____

262. began _____

263. grow _____

264. took _____

265. river _____

266. four _____

267. carry _____

268. state _____

269. once _____

270. book _____

271. hear_____

272. stop _____

273. without _____

274. second_____

275. later _____

276. miss_____

277. idea _____

278. enough_____

279. eat _____

280. face _____

Week 15: 281 - 300

281. watch _____

282. real _____

283. almost _____

284. far _____

285. built _____

286. let _____

287. above _____

288. girl _____

289. sometimes_____

290. mountain_____

291. cut _____

292. young _____

293. talk _____

294. soon _____

295. list _____

296. song _____

297. being _____

298. leave _____

299. family _____

300. it's _____

Week 16: 301 - 320

301. body _____

302. music_____

303. color _____

304. stand _____

305. sun _____

306. questions _____

307. fish _____

308. area _____

309. mark _____

310. dog _____

311. horse _____

312. birds _____

313. problem _____

314. complete _____

315. room _____

316. knew _____

317. since _____

318. ever _____

319. piece _____

320. told _____

Week 17: 321 - 340

321. usually _____

322. didn't _____

323. friends_____

324. easy _____

325. heard _____

326. order _____

327. red _____

328. door _____

329. sure _____

330. become_____

331. top _____

332. ship _____

333. across _____

334. today _____

335. during _____

336. better _____

337. best _____

338. short _____

339. however _____

340. low _____

Week 18: 341 - 360

341. hours _____

342. black _____

343. products_____

344. happened _____

345. whole _____

346. measure _____

347. remember_____

348. early _____

349. waves _____

350. reached _____

351. listen _____

352. wind _____

353. rock_____

354. space _____

355. covered _____

356. fast _____

357. several _____

358. hold _____

359. himself _____

360. toward _____

Week 19: 361 - 380

361. five _____

362. step _____

363. morning _____

364. passed _____

365. vowel _____

366. true _____

367. hundred _____

368. against _____

369. pattern _____

370. numeral _____

371. table _____

372. north _____

373. slowly _____

374. money _____

375. map _____

376. farm _____

377. pulled _____

378. draw _____

379. voice _____

380. seen _____

Week 20: 381 - 400

381. cold _____

382. cried _____

383. plan _____

384. notice _____

385. south _____

386. sing _____

387. war _____

388. ground _____

389. fall _____

390. king _____

391. town _____

392. I'll _____

393. unit _____

394. figure _____

395. certain _____

396. field _____

397. travel _____

398. wood _____

399. fire _____

400. upon _____

Week 21: 401 - 420

401. done _____

402. English _____

403. road _____

404. half _____

405. ten _____

406. fly _____

407. gave _____

408. box _____

409. finally _____

410. wait _____

411. correct _____

412. oh _____

413. quickly _____

414. person _____

415. became _____

416. shown _____

417. minutes _____

418. strong _____

419. verb _____

420. stars _____

Week 22: 421 - 440

421. front _____

422. feel _____

423. fact _____

424. inches_____

425. street _____

426. decided _____

427. contain _____

428. surface _____

429. produce_____

430. building _____

431. ocean _____

432. class _____

433. note _____

434. nothing _____

435. rest _____

436. carefully _____

437. scientists_____

438. inside_____

439. wheels _____

440. stay _____

Week 23: 441 - 460

441. green _____

442. known _____

443. island _____

444. week _____

445. less _____

446. machine _____

447. base _____

448. ago _____

449. stood _____

450. course _____

451. plane _____

452. system _____

453. behind _____

454. boat _____

455. game _____

456. force _____

457. warm _____

458. common _____

459. bring _____

460. though _____

Week 24: 461 - 480

461. language_____

462. shape _____

463. yes _____

464. clear _____

465. ran _____

466. round _____

467. brought _____

468. understand_____

469. explain _____

470. dry _____

471. deep _____

472. thousands _____

473. yet _____

474. government _____

475. able _____

476. filled _____

477. heat _____

478. full _____

479. hot _____

480. check _____

Week 25: 481 - 500

481. object _____

482. am _____

483. rule _____

484. among_____

485. noun _____

486. power _____

487. cannot_____

488. six _____

489. size _____

490. dark _____

491. ball_____

492. material _____

493. special _____

494. heavy _____

495. product _____

496. nation _____

497. pair _____

498. circle _____

499. neighbor_____

500. neighborhood _____

Common Words with Opposite Meanings

It is easier to remember words when you also practice the word with the opposite meaning. The list below has many of the most common English words listed with their opposite meanings.

1. above - below _____

2. add - subtract_____

3. after - before _____

4. all - none _____

5. always - never _____

6. answer - question _____

7, bad - good _____

8. began - ended _____

9. begin - end _____

10. big - little _____

11. black - white _____

12. bottom - top_____

13. boy - girl _____

14. buy - sell _____

15. came - went _____

16, close - open _____

17. arrive - leave _____

18. come - go _____

19. dark - light_____

20. daughter - son _____

21. day - night _____

21. death - life_____

21. die - live _____

24. different - same _____

25. difficult (hard) - easy _____

26. down - up _____

27. dry - wet _____

28. east - west _____

29. early - late _____

30. empty - full _____

31. far - near_____

32. fast - slow _____

33. fat - thin _____

34. father - mother _____

35. few - many _____

36. finish - start_____

37. first - last _____

38. found - lost _____

39. give – take _____

40. peace – war _____

41. front – back _____

42. everything – nothing _____

43. go - stop _____

44. hard – soft_____

45. heavy – light_____

46. high – low _____

47. hot – cold_____

48 in – out _____

49. inside – outside _____

50. large - small_____

51. later – now _____

52. left - right_____

53. less – more_____

54. man – woman_____

55. men – women_____

56. new – old _____

57. no – yes_____

58 north – south _____

59. off – on _____

60. open – shut _____

61. over – under _____

62. part – whole _____

63. right (correct) – wrong _____

64. short – tall _____

65. yesterday – tomorrow _____

66. young – old_____

Vocabulary to Remember

Review: You can write any words that you want to practice on the lines below. You can also write definitions if there were any vocabulary words that you didn't know.

_____

_____

_____

_____

_____

_____

_____

_____

_____

_____

Vocabulary to Remember

Verbs – Past and Present Tense

Every sentence needs to have a verb, so verbs are very important tol learn. It is a good idea to at least know the simple present and past tense for many common verbs. Here are the verbs from the "500 Most Frequently Used Words" and from the USCIS list. They are grouped into regular and irregular verbs for easy practice.

Group A are all Regular verbs. The present tense is regular and the past tense ends in –ed. Group B are all Irregular verbs. They have different endings or a different spelling from their base form.

*If a verb ends with –e and adds –d and there is no other difference from the pattern, it is counted here as a Regular Verb

Example of a Regular Verb

Base verb: answer

Present Tense

I, you, we, they	answer
he, she, it	answers

Past Tense

I, you, he, she, it, we, they	answered

Regular Verbs

Directions: Practice writing commonly used regular verbs on the lines below.

	Present	**Past**
I, you, we, they	he, she, it	(I,you,s/he,it,we,they)
1. answer	answers	answered
2. ask	asks	asked
3. call	calls	called
4. change	changes	changed
5. complete	completes	completed
6. cover	covers	covered
7. explain	explains	explained

Regular Verbs

Present		Past
I, you, we, they	he, she, it	(I,you,s/he,it,we,they)
8. fill	fills	filled
9. help	helps	helped
10. learn	learns	learned
11. like	likes	liked
12. listen	listens	listened
13. live	lives	lived
14. look	looks	looked
15. need	needs	needed

Regular Verbs

Present		Past
I, you, we, they	he, she, it	(I,you,s/he,it,we,they)
16. open	opens	opened
17. pull	pulls	pulled
18. record	records	recorded
19. remember	remember	remembered
20. rent	rents	rented
21. rest	rests	rested
22. save	saves	saved
23. stay	stays	stayed

Regular Verbs

Present		Past
I, you, we, they	he, she, it	(I,you,s/he,it,we,they)
24. travel	travels	traveled
25. turn	turns	turned
26. use	uses	used
27. use	uses	used
28. walk	walks	walked
29. want	wants	wanted
30. work	works	worked

Irregular Verbs

Irregular verbs are more common in English than in many other languages. It will help your writing to know the common irregular verbs above and be able to correctly use them in the present and past tense.

Irregular Verbs

Present		Past
I, you, we, they	he, she, it	(I,you,s/he,it,we,they)
1. become	becomes	became
2. begin	begins	began
3. bring	brings	brought
4. build	builds	built
5. buy	buys	bought
6. carry	carries	carried

Irregular Verbs

Present		Past
I, you, we, they	he, she, it	(I,you,s/he,it,we,they)
7. come	comes	came
8. cry	cries	cried
9. cut	cuts	cut
10. draw	draw	drew
11. eat	eats	ate
12. feel	feels	felt
13. find	finds	found
14. fly	flies	flew

Irregular Verbs

Present		Past
I, you, we, they	he, she, it	(I,you,s/he,it,we,they)
15. get	gets	got
16. give	gives	gave
17. go	goes	went
18. grow	grows	grew
19. hold	holds	held
20. know	knows	knew
21. leave	leaves	left
22. make	makes	made

Irregular Verbs

Present		Past
I, you, we, they	he, she, it	(I,you,s/he,it,we,they)
23. pass	passes	passed
24. plan	plans	planned
25. put	puts	put
26. reach	reaches	reached
27. read	reads	read
28. run	runs	ran
29. say	says	said
36. see	sees	saw

Irregular Verbs

Present		Past
I, you, we, they	he, she, it	(I,you,s/he,it,we,they)
37. sing	sings	sang
38. stand	stands	stood
39. stop	stops	stopped
40. study	studies	studied
41. take	takes	took
42. teach	teaches	taught
43. tell	tells	told
44. think	thinks	thought

Irregular Verbs

Present		Past
I, you, we, they	he, she, it	(I,you,s/he,it,we,they)
45. try	tries	tried
46. understand	understands	understood
47. write	writes	wrote

For More Practice

_____

_____

_____

_____

_____

_____

_____

_____

_____

_____

The verb "be" is very often used and is very irregular. This is an important verb to practice and use correctly, in both the present and past tense.

A Tip!

Know this Important Irregular Verb:

be

present tense		**past tense**	
I	am	I	was
you, we, they	are	you, we, they	were
he, she, it	is	he, she, it	was

Try it yourself! Write the correct form and tense of "be" on the line in the sentences on the next page. Correct your sentences and then read each sentence aloud to practice your reading and pronunciation.

You can hear the sentences correctly pronounced on an audio link at the "Welcome ESL" website: **www.welcomeesl.com**

Can you complete these sentences with the correct form of the verb "be"? (The answers are at the bottom of the page.)

Using the Irregular Verb "be"

1. I _____ an American.

2. _____ you a student now?

3. No, I _____ a student last year.

4. She _____ learning English now.

5. They _____ at home yesterday.

6. _____ he at work last Friday?

7. The President and First Lady _____ in New York.

8. Today _____ a sunny day.

9. She _____ at the market now.

10. I _____ at work early every day last week.

Answers: 1. am   2. Are   3. was   4. is   5. were
6. Was   7. were   8. is ("was" could also be correct if you are thinking that it is now night and the day is over.)
9. Are   10. was

Difficult Verbs to Remember

_____

_____

_____

_____

_____

_____

_____

_____

_____

_____

_____

_____

_____

_____

_____

_____

_____

13

Practice Sentences

More Reading and Writing Practice

Famous People in American History

Joe Biden
Vice-President of the United States

Civics Test Question #29: What is the name of the vice-President of the United States now?

Answer: (Joe) Biden

13

Practice Sentences
More Reading and Writing

First, read each sentence aloud for reading practice. Then write (copy) the sentence on the line below.

Circle the number in front of any sentence that is difficult for you to write. Ask a friend to read it to you and, without looking at the original, write the sentence that you hear on a piece of paper.

Be sure to print or handwrite neatly. (Printing is easier for the USCIS officer to read).

Remember:

What does every sentence begin with?
Answer: A capital letter.

What does every sentence end with?
Answer: A period or a question mark.

Don't forget to capitalize names and places.
The word is incorrect if it is not capitalized correctly.

A Tip!

Tip: Pay attention to the sentences you are asked to read at your citizenship test. Sometimes a USCIS officer will ask you to write those same sentences on your writing test.

Practice Sentences to Read and Write

1. Washington, D.C. is the capital of the United States.

_____

_____

2. Lincoln was President during the Civil War.

_____

_____

3. Mexico is south of California.

_____

_____

4. The American flag is red, white and blue.

_____

_____

5. Today is Independence Day.

_____

_____

6. People elect 100 senators.

_____

_____

7. Today is a sunny day.

_____

8. Alaska is the largest state.

_____

_____

9. One important right in America is freedom of speech.

_____

_____

10. There are 50 states.

_____

_____

11. Tuesday was a rainy day, but today is cloudy.

_____

_____

12. People come here from many different countries.

_____

_____

13. Some people want to become U.S. citizens.

_____

14. After we ate dinner, we went to night school.

_____

_____

_____

More Practice Sentences
for Reading and Writing

USCIS does not tell you the sentences or vocabulary that they will use on the reading and writing tests, and they often change them. The sentences below use many of the words on the USCIS reading and writing vocabulary lists. They also use many of the helpful bonus words. You can read them to someone out loud for extra reading practice and then have someone read them to you to practice your writing.

Tip: Remember to have someone else always correct your writing, if possible. It is easy to not see your own mistakes.

1. Yesterday was Wednesday.

_____

_____

2. Lincoln was president during the Civil War.

_____

_____

3. How many colors are in the flag of the United States?

_____

_____

4. There are fifty states in this country.

_____

5. Freedom of speech is an important right.

_____

_____

6. President Obama lives in the White House.

_____

_____

7. Washington, D.C. is the capital of the United States.

_____

_____

8. Mexico is south of the United States.

_____

_____

9. Many people came from Canada to live here.

_____

_____

10. Thanksgiving is always in November.

_____

_____

11. The three colors of the American flag are red, white and blue.

_____

_____

12. Voters elect two senators from every state.

_____

_____

13. The largest state is Alaska.

_____

_____

14. Independence Day is in July.

_____

_____

15. The U.S. Congress makes laws.

_____

_____

16. People pay taxes every year in April.

_____

_____

17. American citizens are free to vote.

_____

_____

18. Tomorrow is the first day of June.

_____

_____

19. You can meet my family today.

_____

_____

20. Do you like your job?

_____

_____

21. She works hard every morning and night.

_____

_____

22. The children went to school early today.

_____

_____

23. What time do you go to sleep?

_____

_____

24. Where does he go after work?

_____

_____

25. When she comes home, she likes to use the computer.

_____

_____

26. Dogs are very different from cats.

_____

_____

27. Could you please repeat that question?

_____

_____

28. Did you ask for his address and phone number?

_____

_____

29. Remember to bring all your papers to the meeting.

_____

_____

30. This book is very interesting and helpful.

_____

_____

33. Will you give me your letter now or later?

_____

_____

32. They will begin a new business in February.

_____

_____

31. I think English is an important language, but it is very
    difficult to learn.

_____

_____

_____

32. I want to become a citizen because I like to live in the
    United States.

_____

_____

A Tip!

Tip: Many civics questions list more than one correct answer. Usually, you only need to know one of the answers. If you need to know more, the question will tell you how many answers you need to know. (For example, Question #9 asks you to, "Name two rights in the Declaration of Independence".)

14

The Civics Questions

Famous Places in America

The White House
1600 Pennsylvania Avenue NW, Washington, D.C. 20500

Civics Test Question #94: What is the capital of the United States?

Answer: Washington, D.C.

14

100 Civics Questions and Answers

American Government

A: Principles of American Democracy

1. **What is the supreme law of the land?**

   the Constitution

2. **What does the Constitution do? (know one)**

   - sets up the government
   - defines the government
   - protects basic rights of Americans

3. **The idea of self-government is in the first three words of the Constitution. What are these words?**

   We the People

4. **What is an amendment?**

   - a change (to the Constitution)
   - an addition (to the Constitution)

5. **What do we call the first ten amendments to the Constitution?**

   - the Bill of Rights

6. What is one right or freedom from the First Amendment?*

- speech
- religion
- assembly
- press
- petition the government

7. How many amendments does the Constitution have?

twenty-seven (27)

8. What did the Declaration of Independence do?

- announced our independence (from Great Britain)
- declared our independence (from Great Britain)
- said that the United States is free (from Great Britain)

9. What are two rights in the Declaration of Independence?

- life
- liberty
- pursuit of happiness

10. **What is freedom of religion?**

You can practice any religion, or not practice (have) a religion.

11. **What is the economic system in the United States?***

- capitalist economy
- market economy

12. **What is the "rule of law"?**

- Everyone must follow the law.
- Leaders must obey the law.
- Government must obey the law.
- No one is above the law.

B: System of Government

13. **Name one branch or part of the government.***

- Congress
- legislative
- President
- executive
- the courts
- judicial

14. **What stops one branch of government from becoming too powerful?**

- checks and balances
- separation of powers

15. Who is in charge of the executive branch?

the President

16. Who makes federal laws?

- Congress
- Senate and House (of Representatives)
- (U.S. or national) legislature

17. What are the two parts of the U.S. Congress?*

the Senate and House (of Representatives)

18. How many U.S. Senators are there?

one hundred (100)

19. We elect a U.S. Senator for how many years?

six (6)

20. Who is one of your state's U.S. Senators now?*

•Answers will be different for each state. Check the internet www.senate.gov for the current names in your state. [District of Columbia residents and residents of U.S. territories should answer that D.C.—or the territory where the applicant lives—has no U.S. Senators.]

21. The House of Representatives has how many voting members?

four hundred thirty-five (435)

22. We elect a U.S. Representative for how many years?

two (2)

23. Name your U.S. Representative.

▪Answers will be different for each area. See the website: www.house.gov for the newest names.

[Residents of territories with non-voting Delegates or Resident Commissioners may provide the name of that Delegate or Commissioner. Also acceptable is any statement that the territory has no (voting) Representatives in Congress.]

24. Who does a U.S. Senator represent?

all people of the state

25. Why do some states have more Representatives than other states?

- (because of) the state's population
- (because) they have more people
- (because) some states have more people

26. We elect a President for how many years?

four (4)

27. In what month do we vote for President?*

November

28. What is the name of the President of the United States now?*

- Barack Obama
- Obama

29. What is the name of the Vice President of the United States now?

- Joseph R. Biden, Jr.
- Joe Biden
- Biden

30. If the President can no longer serve, who becomes President?

the Vice President

31. If both the President and the Vice President can no longer serve, who becomes President?

the Speaker of the House

32. Who is the Commander in Chief of the military?

the President

33. Who signs bills to become laws?

the President

34. Who vetoes bills?

the President

35. What does the President's Cabinet do?

advises the President

36. What are two Cabinet-level positions?

- Vice President
- Attorney General
- Secretary of Agriculture
- Secretary of Commerce
- Secretary of Defense
- Secretary of Education
- Secretary of Energy
- Secretary of Health and Human Services
- Secretary of Homeland Security
- Secretary of Housing and Urban Development
- Secretary of the Interior
- Secretary of Labor
- Secretary of State
- Secretary of Transportation
- Secretary of the Treasury
- Secretary of Veterans Affairs

37. What does the judicial branch do?

- reviews laws
- explains laws
- resolves disputes (disagreements)
- decides if a law goes against the
     Constitution

38. What is the highest court in the United States?

the Supreme Court

39. How many justices are on the Supreme Court?

nine (9)

40. Who is the Chief Justice of the United States now? (Know one way to say his name).

- John Roberts
- John G. Roberts, Jr.

41. Under our Constitution, some powers belong to the federal government. What is one power of the federal government?

- to print money
- to declare war
- to create an army
- to make treaties

42. Under our Constitution, some powers belong to the states. What is one power of the states?

- provide schooling and education
- provide protection (police)
- provide safety (fire departments)
- give a driver's license
- approve zoning and land use

43. Who is the governor of your state now?

▪Answers will be different for each state. [District of Columbia residents should answer that D.C. does not have a governor.]

44. What is the capital of your state?*

The States and the State Capitals

Alabama - Montgomery	Kansas - Topeka
Alaska - Juneau	Kentucky - Frankfort
Arizona - Phoenix	Louisiana - Baton Rouge
Arkansas - Little Rock	Maine - Augusta
California - Sacramento	Maryland - Annapolis
Colorado - Denver	Massachusetts - Boston
Connecticut - Hartford	Michigan - Lansing
Delaware - Dover	Minnesota - St. Paul
Florida - Tallahassee	Mississippi - Jackson
Georgia - Atlanta	Missouri - Jefferson City
Hawaii - Honolulu	Montana - Helena
Idaho - Boise	Nebraska - Lincoln
Illinois - Springfield	Nevada - Carson City
Indiana - Indianapolis	New Hampshire - Concord
Iowa - Des Moines	New Jersey - Trenton

New Mexico - Santa Fe
New York - Albany
North Carolina - Raleigh
North Dakota - Bismarck
Ohio - Columbus
Oklahoma - Oklahoma City
Oregon - Salem
Pennsylvania - Harrisburg
Rhode Island - Providence
South Carolina - Columbia

South Dakota - Pierre
Tennessee - Nashville
Texas - Austin
Utah - Salt Lake City
Vermont - Montpelier
Virginia - Richmond
Washington - Olympia
West Virginia - Charleston
Wisconsin - Madison
Wyoming - Cheyenne

[District of Columbia residents should answer that D.C. is not a state and does not have a capital. Residents of U.S. territories should name the capital of the territory.]

45. What are the two major political parties in the United States?*

Democratic and Republican

46. What is the political party of the President now?

Democratic (Party)

47. What is the name of the Speaker of the House of Representatives now?

(John) Boehner

C: Rights and Responsibilities

48. There are four amendments to the Constitution about who can vote. Describe one of them.

- Citizens eighteen (18) and older (can vote).
- You don't have to pay (a poll tax) to vote.
- Any citizen can vote. (Women and men can vote.)
- A male citizen of any race (can vote).

49. What is one responsibility that is only for United States citizens?*

- serve on a jury
- vote in a federal election

50. Name one right only for United States citizens.

- vote in a federal election
- run for federal office

51. What are two rights of everyone living in the United States?

- freedom of expression
- freedom of speech
- freedom of assembly
- freedom to petition the government
- freedom of worship
- the right to bear arms

52. What do we show loyalty to when we say the Pledge of Allegiance?

- the United States
- the flag

53. What is one promise you make when you become a United States citizen?

- to give up loyalty to other countries
- to defend the Constitution and laws of the United States
- to obey the laws of the United States
- to serve in the U.S. military (if needed)
- to serve (do important work for) the nation (if needed)
- to be loyal to the United States

54. How old do citizens have to be to vote for President?*

eighteen (18) and older

55. What are two ways that Americans can participate in their democracy?

- vote
- join a political party
- help with a campaign
- join a civic group
- join a community group
- give an elected official your opinion on an issue
- call Senators and Representatives
- publicly support or oppose an issue or policy
- run for office write to a newspaper

56. When is the last day you can send in federal income tax forms?*

April 15

57. When must all men register for the Selective Service?

- at age eighteen (18)
- between eighteen (18) and twenty-six (26)

The Selective Service

American History

A: Colonial Period and Independence

58. What is one reason colonists came to America?

- freedom
- political liberty
- religious freedom
- economic opportunity
- practice their religion
- escape persecution

59. Who lived in America before the Europeans arrived?
- American Indians
- Native Americans

60. What group of people was taken to America and sold as slaves?

- Africans
- people from Africa

61. Why did the colonists fight the British?

- because of high taxes ("taxation without representation")
- because the British army stayed in their - houses (boarding, quartering)
- because they didn't have self-government

62. Who wrote the Declaration of Independence?

(Thomas) Jefferson

63. When was the Declaration of Independence adopted?

July 4, 1776

64. There were 13 original states. Name three.

Connecticut	New York
Delaware	North Carolina
Georgia	Pennsylvania
Maryland	Rhode Island
Massachusetts	South Carolina
New Hampshire	Virginia
New Jersey	

65. What happened at the Constitutional Convention?

- The Constitution was written.
- The Founding Fathers wrote the Constitution.

66. When was the Constitution written?

1787

67. The Federalist Papers supported the passage of the U.S. Constitution. Name one of the writers.

- (James) Madison
- (Alexander) Hamilton
- (John) Jay
- Publius

68. What is one thing Benjamin Franklin is famous for?

- U.S. diplomat
- oldest member of the Constitutional Convention
- first Postmaster General of the United States
- writer of "Poor Richard's Almanac"
- started the first free libraries

69. Who is the "Father of Our Country"?

(George) Washington

70. Who was the first President?*

(George) Washington

George Washington,
the First U.S. President

B: 1800s

71. What territory did the United States but from France in 1803?

- the Louisiana Territory
- Louisiana

72. Name one war fought by the United States in the 1800s.

- War of 1812
- Mexican-American War
- Civil War
- Spanish-American War

73. Name the U.S. war between the North and the South. (Both are correct ways to say the name of this war. You need to remember one of them.)

- the Civil War
- the War between the States

74. Name one problem that led to the Civil War.

- slavery
- economic reasons
- states' rights

75. What was one important thing that Abraham Lincoln did?*

-freed the slaves (Emancipation Proclamation)
-saved (or preserved) the Union
-led the United States during the Civil War

**Abraham Lincoln,
President during the Civil War**

76. **What did the Emancipation Proclamation do?**

-freed the slaves
-freed slaves in the Confederacy
-freed slaves in the Confederate states
-freed slaves in most Southern states

77. **What did Susan B. Anthony do?**

-fought for women's rights
-fought for civil rights

C: Recent American History and Other Important Historical Information

78. **Name one war fought by the United States in the 1900s.***

-World War I
-World War II
-Korean War
-Vietnam War
-(Persian) Gulf War

79. **Who was President during World War I?**

(Woodrow) Wilson

80. Who was President during the Great Depression and World War II?

(Franklin) Roosevelt

81. Who did the United States fight in World War II?

Japan, Germany, and Italy

82. Before he was President, Eisenhower was a general. What war was he in?

World War II

83. During the Cold War, what was the main concern of the United States?

Communism

84. What movement tried to end racial discrimination?

civil rights (movement)

85. What did Martin Luther King, Jr. do?*

-fought for civil rights
-worked for equality for all Americans

86. What major event happened on September 11, 2001, in the United States?

-Terrorists attacked the United States.

87. Name one American Indian tribe in the United States.

[USCIS Officers will be supplied with a list of federally recognized American Indian tribes.]

Pueblo	Navajo
Seminole	Cherokee
Creek	Apache
Sioux	Shawnee
Chippewa	Mohegan
Choctaw	Iroquois
Blackfeet	Cheyenne
Arawak	Inuit
Huron	Crow
Oneida	Lakota
Hopi	Teton

Integrated Civics

A: Geography

88. Name one of the two longest rivers in the United States.

-Missouri (River)
-Mississippi (River)

89. What ocean is on the West Coast of the United States?

Pacific (Ocean)

90. What ocean is on the East Coast of the United States?

Atlantic (Ocean)

91. Name one U.S. territory.

- Puerto Rico
- U.S. Virgin Islands
- American Samoa
- Northern Mariana Islands
- Guam

92. Name one state that borders Canada.

Maine	Minnesota
New Hampshire	North Dakota
Vermont	Montana
New York	Idaho
Pennsylvania	Washington
Ohio	Alaska
Michigan	

93. Name one state that borders Mexico.

- California
- Arizona
- New Mexico
- Texas

94. What is the capital of the United States?*

Washington, D.C.

95. Where is the Statue of Liberty?* (The answers are two names for the same place. Remember one of these.)

- New York (Harbor)
- Liberty Island

[Also acceptable are "New Jersey", "near New York City", or "on the Hudson (River)".]

The Statue of Liberty

B: Symbols

96. Why does the flag have 13 stripes?

- because there were 13 original colonies
- because the stripes represent the original colonies

97. Why does the flag have 50 stars?*

- because there is one star for each state
- because each star represents a state
- because there are 50 states

98. What is the name of the national anthem?

The Star-Spangled Banner

C: Holidays

99. When do we celebrate Independence Day?*

July 4

100. Name two national U.S. holidays.

- New Year's Day
- Martin Luther King, Jr. Day
- Presidents' Day
- Memorial Day
- Independence Day
- Labor Day
- Columbus Day
- Veterans Day
- Thanksgiving
- Christmas

Independence Day, July 4th

Veteran's Day, 2011. President Obama and General Michael Linnington walk to the Tomb of the Unknown Soldiers at Arlington Cemetery on Veteran's Day, November 11, 2011

15

Civics Questions Practice - Multiple Choice

Reminder: At your citizenship interview, the civics questions will not be multiple choice. You will need to know the answer to 6 out of 10 questions to pass. The USCIS officer will choose the questions from the 100 questions and answers in Chapter 14.

The civics test is oral, and is not multiple choice. But these multiple choice questions are good practice. Completing them can help you remember the answers when the USCIS officer asks.

National Anthem of the United States

The Star Spangled Banner
written by Francis Scott Key (1814)

Oh, say can you see by the dawn's early light
What so proudly we hailed
at the twilight's last gleaming?
Whose broad stripes and bright stars
thru the perilous fight
O'er the ramparts
were so gallantly streaming?
And the rocket's red glare,
the bombs bursting in air,
Gave proof through the night
that our flag was still there.
Oh, say does that star-spangled banner yet wave
O'er the land of the free and the home of the
    brave?

Civics Test Question #98: What is the name of the national anthem?

Answer: "The Star-Spangled Banner

15

Civics Multiple Choice Practice

Directions: Read each civics question below, and circle the letter of the correct answer.

1. What is the supreme law of the land?

a. the Supreme Court
b. the President
c. the Declaration of Independence
d. the Constitution

2. What does the Constitution do?

a. sets up the government
b. explains the Declaration of Independence
c. limits immigration
d. describes the nation's freedom from England

3. The idea of self-government is in the first three words of the Constitution. What are these words?

a. Congress shall make
b. We the People
c. We the Colonists
d. All men are created equal

4. What is an amendment?

a. the beginning of the Declaration of Independence
b. the Preamble to the Constitution
c. a change to the Constitution
d. an introduction

5. What do we call the first ten amendments to the Constitution?

a. the Declaration of Independence
b. the Bill of Rights
c. the inalienable rights
d. the Articles of Confederation

6. What is one right or freedom in the First Amendment?

a. to bear arms
b. to vote
c. speech
d. trial by jury

7. How many amendments does the Constitution have?

a. 10
b. 15
c. 22
d. 27

8. What does the Declaration of Independence do?

a. say that all Americans are independent from the government
b. separate colonial Americans from Great Britain in a new country
c. declare colonial America is independent of Canada
d. declare American independence from France

9. What are two rights in the Declaration of Independence?

a. the right to happiness and a good job
b. liberty and an independent government
c. liberty and the pursuit of happiness
d. wealth and good health

10. What is freedom of religion?

a. You must choose a religion.
b. You can choose to be any religion you want to, or not have a religion and the government will not interfere with your choice.
c. You can choose the time you observe your religion.
d. You do not need to pay to join a church or temple.

11. What is the economic system of the United States?

a. socialism
b. capitalism
c. democracy
d. communism

12. What is the rule of law?

a. Everyone must follow the law.
b. Everyone but the President must follow the law.
c. the president rules by laws
d. All laws must be the same in every state.

13. Name one branch of government

a. the Supreme Court
b. executive
c. House of Representatives
d. state governments

14. What stops any branch of government from becoming too powerful?

a. checks and balances
b. the power of the Presidency
c. the voters
d. freedom of speech

15. Who is in charge of the executive branch?

a. President
b. Secretary of Defense
c. Vice President
d. Congress

16. Who makes federal laws?

a. the Supreme Court
b. the President
c. Congress
d. the states

17. What are the two parts to the U.S. Congress?

a. the Supreme Court and the lower courts
b. the Senate and all the state governors
c. the House of Lords and the House of Commons
d. the Senate and House of Representatives

18. How many U.S. senators are there?

a. 50
b. 2
c. 100
d. 200

19. We elect a U.S. Senator for how many years?

a. ten (10)
b. two (2)
c. four (4)
d. six (6)

20. Who is one of your state's senators?

_____

21. How many voting members does the House of Representatives have?

a. 100
b. 200
c. 435
d. 365

22. We elect a U.S. Representative for how many years?

a. eight (8)
b. four (4)
c. six (6)
d. two (2)

23. Name your representative.

_____

24. Who does a U.S. Senator represent?

a. the state legislatures
b. all people of the state
c. only the people in the state who voted for the Senator
d. all people of the state who belong to the Senator's political party.

25. Why do some states have more representatives than others?

a. larger states get more representatives
b. representatives are based on state population
c. states that have been in the U.S. longer have more representatives
d. small states do not have many representatives

26. We elect a President for how many years?

a. four (4)
b. two (2)
c. ten (10)
d. eight (8)

27. In what month do we elect a president?

a. July
b. November
c. January
d. October

28. Who is the President now?

a. Joe Obama
b. Joe Biden
c. George Washington
d. Barack Obama

29. Who is the Vice President now?

a. Joe Biden
b. Hilary Clinton
c. Barack Obama
d. Thomas Jefferson

30. If the President can no longer serve, who becomes President?

a. the President Pro-Tempore
b. the Secretary of State
c. the Vice President
d. the President

31. If both the President and the Vice President can no longer serve, who becomes President?

a. the Speaker of the House
b. the Secretary of State
c. the Vice President
d. the Secretary of Defense

32. Who is the Commander in Chief of the military?

a. the Vice President
b. the President
c. the Secretary of State
d. the Secretary of Defense

33. Who signs the bills to make them into laws?

a. the President
b. the vice-President
c. the Speaker of the House
d. the President of the Senate

34. Who vetoes bills?

a. the Vice President
b. the President
c. the Speaker of the House
d. the President Pro Tempore

35. What does the President's cabinet do?

a. writes the yearly budget to submit to Congress
b. approves presidential appointments
c. advises the President
d. works closely with Congress

36. What are two Cabinet-level positions?

a. Secretary of Homeland Security and Secretary of the Treasury
b. Secretary of Health and Human Services and Secretary of the Navy
c. Secretary of Weather and Secretary of Energy
d. Secretary of the Interior and Secretary of History

37. What does the judicial branch do?

a. reviews and explains laws
b. appoints judges
c. makes laws
d. choose Supreme Court judges

38. What is the highest court in the country?

a. the Appeals Court
b. the Supreme Court
c. superior courts
d. district courts

39. How many justices are on the Supreme Court?

a. nine (9)
b. ten (10)
c. eleven (11)
d. twelve (12)

40. Who is the Chief Justice of the United States now?

a. Joe Biden
b. Barack Obama
c. John G. Roberts, Jr.
d. Anthony Kennedy

41. Under our Constitution, some powers belong to the federal government. What is one power of the federal government?

a. to make treaties
b. to provide police departments
c. to provide schooling
d. to issue driver's licenses

42. The Constitution gives powers to the states. Which of the following is not a state power:

a. gives drivers licenses
b. collects taxes
c. prints money
d. provides safety (police and fire departments)

43. Who is your governor?

_____

Check online at: www.usa.gov

44. What is your state capital?

_____

Check online at: www.usa.gov

45. What are the two major political parties in the United States?

a. American and Bull-Moose
b. Democratic and Republican
c. Democratic-Republican and Whigs
d. Libertarian and Green

46. What is the political party of the President now?

a. Republican Party
b. Democratic Party
c. Independent Party
d. Green Party

47. What is the name of the current (2013) Speaker of the House?

a. Joe Biden
b. John Boehner
c. Nancy Pelosi
d. Harry Reid

48. There are four amendments to the Constitution about voting. Describe one of them.

a. Citizens eighteen (18) and older can vote.
b. Citizens seventeen (17) and older can vote.
c. Only citizens with a job can vote.
d. Only citizens by birth can vote.

49. Which of the following is not a responsibility for all U.S. citizens?

a. serve on a jury
b. get a passport
c. vote
d. pay taxes

50. Which of the following rights is only for U.S. citizens?

a. pay taxes
b. get medical care
c. go to college
d. vote

51. Which two rights are for citizens <u>and</u> non-citizens living in the U.S.?

a. freedom of speech and the right to vote
b. freedom of speech and serving on a jury
c. freedom of speech and freedom of religion
d. the right to vote and the right to travel on a U.S. passport

52. What do we show loyalty to when we say the Pledge of Allegiance?

a. the Founding Fathers
b. the United States
c. the Constitution
d. the U.S. military

53. What is one promise that you make when you become a U.S. citizen?

a. to bring your family to the United States
b. to get an American passport
c. to get a driver's license
d. to be loyal to the United States

54. How old do citizens need to be to vote?

a. 21
b. 18
c. 25
d. 20

55. What are two ways that Americans can participate in their democracy?

a. vote and join a civic group
b. give an elected official your opinion on an issue and join a community group
c. all of these answers
d. write to a newspaper and call Senators and Representatives

56. When is the last day you can send in federal income tax forms?

a. July 4
b. March 15
c. May 15
d. April 15

57. When must all men register for the Selective Service?

a. between eighteen (18) and twenty-six (26)
b. at any age
c. only at age eighteen (18)
d. men do not have to register

58. Why did colonists come to America?

a. for religious freedom
b. for political freedom
c. for economic opportunities
d. all of the above

59. Who lived in America before the Europeans arrived?

a. no one
b. Floridians
c. American Indians
d. Canadians

60. What group of people was taken to America and sold as slaves?

a. English
b. Canadians
c. Dutch
d. Africans

61. Why did the colonists fight the British?

a. because they didn't have self-government
b. all of these answers
c. because the British army stayed in their houses
d. because of high taxes

62 Who wrote the Declaration of Independence?

a. George Washington
b. Thomas Jefferson
c. Benjamin Franklin
d. James Madison

63. When was the Declaration of Independence adopted?

a. July 4, 1776
b. January 1, 1775
c. December 10, 1776
d. July 1, 1775

64. There were 13 original states. Which of the following were included?

a. Georgia, Maine, Texas
b. New Hampshire, New York, New Mexico
c. Rhode Island, Delaware, Washington, D.C.
d. Georgia, Pennsylvania, New York

65. What happened at the Constitutional Convention?

a. The Constitution was presented to King George
b. The Constitution was written.
c. They wrote the Bill of Rights
d. They drafted the Declaration of Independence

66. When was the Constitution written?

a. 1776
b. 1787
c. 1789
d. 1790

67. The Federalist Papers supported the passage of the U.S. Constitution. Name one writer.

a. John Adams
b. George Washington
c. James Madison
d. Thomas Jefferson

68. What is one thing Benjamin Franklin is famous for?

a. youngest member of the Constitutional Convention
b. third President of the United States
c. U.S. diplomat
d. all of the above

69. Who is "The Father of Our Country"?

a. George Washington
b. Barack Obama
c. Franklin Roosevelt
d. Abraham Lincoln

70. Who was the first president of the United States?

a. Thomas Jefferson
b. George Washington
c. James Madison
d. John Adams

71. What territory did the United States buy from France in 1803?

a. Quebec
b. Haiti
c. Alaska
d. the Louisiana Territory

72. Name one war fought by the U.S. in the 1800s.

a. World War II
b. Civil War
c. Korean War
d. World War I

73. Name the U.S. war between the northern and southern states.

a. the Civil War
b. the American Revolution
c. the War of 1812
d. the Vietnam War

74. Which of these problems led to the Civil War?

a. slavery
b. economic conflicts
c. international treaties
d. a and b

75. What was one important thing that Abraham Lincoln did?

a. established the United Nations
b. saved (or preserved) the Union
c. lead the U.S. to victory in World War I
d. purchased Alaska

76. What did the Emancipation Proclamation do?

a. ended World War I
b. ended the Civil War
c. gave women the right to vote
d. freed the slaves

77. Which of the following fought for women's rights in the U.S.?

a. Emily Dickenson
b. Martha Washington
c. Susan B. Anthony
d. Jenny Lind

78. Name one war fought by the U.S. in the 1900s.

a. the Korean war
b. the French-Indian War
c. the Spanish-American War
d. the Mexican-American War

79. Who was President during World War I?

a. Theodore Roosevelt
b. Franklin Roosevelt
c. Woodrow Wilson
d. Warren Harding

80. Who was President during World War II?

a. Woodrow Wilson
b. Franklin Roosevelt
c. Theodore Roosevelt
d. Warren Harding

81. Which country did the U.S. fight in WWII?

a. Japan
b. Germany
c. Italy
d. all of the above

82. Before he was President, Eisenhower was a general. What war was he in?

a. Civil War
b. World War II
c. Spanish-American War
d. Vietnam War

83. During the Cold War, what was the main concern of the United States?

a. the Great Depression
b. climate change
c. Communism
d. slavery

84. What movement tried to end racial discrimination?

a. civil rights movement
b. conservation
c. prohibition
d   women's suffrage

85. What did Martin Luther King, Jr. do?

a. fought for civil rights
b. led the nation through World War II
c. was the first African-American Secretary of State
d. wrote the Declaration of Independence

86. What major event happened on September 11, 2001, in the United States?

a. Hurricane Andrew struck the United States.
b. The accident at Three Mile Island Nuclear Power Plant occurred.
c. Terrorists attacked the United States.
d. The Japanese attacked Pearl Harbor.

87. Which of the following is not an American Indian tribe?

a. Celts
b. Cherokee
c. Crow
d. Apache

88. Which of the following is the longest river in the U.S.?

a. the Columbia river
b. the Missouri river
c. the Colorado river
d. the Hudson river

89. What ocean is on the West Coast of the United States?

a. Arctic Ocean
b. Indian Ocean
c. Pacific Ocean
d. Atlantic Ocean

90. What ocean is on the East Coast of the United States?

a. Arctic Ocean
b. Indian Ocean
c. Pacific Ocean
d. Atlantic Ocean

91. Which of the following is not a U.S. territory?

a. Guam
b. Okinawa
c. Puerto Rico
d. American Samoa

92. Name one state that borders Canada.

a. Rhode Island
b. South Dakota
c. Maine
d. Oregon

93. What state borders Mexico?

a. Kansas
b. Texas
c. Utah
d. Washington

94. What is the capitol of U.S.?

a. Washington, D.C.
b. New York City, NY
c. Hollywood, California
d. Boston, Massachusetts

95. Where is the Statue of Liberty?

a. Long Island
b. New York Harbor
c. San Francisco Bay
d. Boston Harbor

96. Why does the flag have 13 stripes?

a. because the stripes represent the members of the Second Continental Congress
b. because it was considered lucky to have 13 stripes on the flag
c. because the stripes represent the original colonies
d. because the stripes represent the number of signatures on the U.S. Constitution.

97. Why does the flag have 50 stars?

a. for the 50 original Founding Fathers
b. for the 50 states
c. for the original 50 colonies
d. for the 50 departments in the federal government

98. What is the U.S. national anthem?

a. "Stars and Stripes Forever"
b. "America, the Beautiful"
c. "The Star-Spangled Banner"
d. "My Country 'Tis of Thee"

99. When do we celebrate Independence Day?

a. July 4
b. January 1
c. October 31
d. April 15

100. Which of the following are not two official national holidays?

a. Christmas and Thanksgiving
b. Presidents' Day and Columbus Day
c. Veteran's Day and Memorial Day
d. Valentine's Day and Halloween

Answers:

1. d. the Constitution
2. a. sets up the government
3. b. We the People
4. c. a change to the Constitution
5. b. the Bill of Rights
6. c. speech
7. d. 27
8. b. separate colonial Americans from Great Britain in a new country
9. c. liberty and the pursuit of happiness
10. b. You can choose to be any religion you want to, or not have a religion and the government will not interfere with your choice.
11. b. capitalism
12. a. Everyone must follow the law.
13. b. executive
14. a. checks and balances
15. a. President
16. c. Congress
17. d. the Senate and House of Representatives
18. c. 100
19. d. six (6)
20. Answers will vary.
21. c. 435
22. d. two (2)
23. Answers will vary.
24. b. all people of the state
25. b. representatives are based on state population
26. a. four (4)
27. b. November
28. d. Barack Obama

29. a. Joe Biden
30. c. the Vice President
31. a. the Speaker of the House
32. b. the President
33. a. the President
34. b. the President
35. c. advises the President
36. a. Secretary of Homeland Security and Secretary of the Treasury
37. a. reviews and explains laws
38. b. the Supreme Court
39. a. nine (9)
40. c. John G. Roberts, Jr.
41. a. to make treaties
42. c. prints money
43. Answers will vary.
44. Answers will vary.
45. b. Democratic and Republican
46. b. Democratic Party
47. b. John Boehner
48. a. Citizens eighteen (18) and older can vote.
49. b. get a passport
50. d. vote
51. c. freedom of speech and freedom of religion
52. b. the United States
53. d. to be loyal to the United States
54. b. 18
55. c. all of these answers
56. d. April 15
57. a. between eighteen (18) and twenty-six (26)
58. d. all of the above
59. c. American Indians
60. d. Africans

61. b. all of these answers
62. b. Thomas Jefferson
63. a. July 4, 1776
64. d. Georgia, Pennsylvania, New York
65. b. The Constitution was written.
66. b. 1787
67. c. James Madison
68. c. U.S. diplomat
69. a. George Washington
70 b. George Washington
71. d. the Louisiana Territory
72. b. Civil War
73. a. the Civil War
74. d. (a and b)
75. b. saved (or preserved) the Union
76. d. freed the slaves
77. c. Susan B. Anthony
78. a. the Korean war
79. c. Woodrow Wilson
80. b. Franklin Roosevelt
81. d. all of the above
82. b. World War II
83. c. Communism
84. a. civil rights movement
85. a. fought for civil rights
86. c. Terrorists attacked the United States.
87. a. Celts
88. b. the Missouri river
89. c. Pacific Ocean
90. d. Atlantic Ocean
91. b. Okinawa

92. c. Maine
93. b. Texas
94. a. Washington, D.C.
95. b. New York Harbor
96. c. because the stripes represent the original colonies
97. b. for the 50 states
98. c. "The Star-Spangled Banner"
99. a. July 4
100. d. Valentine's Day and Halloween

16

Civics Questions Only - For Easier Review
How Many Answers Do You Already Know?

Famous Symbols of America

The Statue of Liberty
detail from a painting by Edward Moran

Civics Test Question #95: Where is the Statue of Liberty?

Answer: Liberty Island (or New York Harbor)

16

Civics Questions Only - For Easier Review
How Many Answers Do You Already Know?

Study Tip: To see how many answers you already know, you can try 10-20 questions a day and mark a "?" (using a pencil) next to the number of any question that you do not know. Then look it up on the flashcards at the back of this book, beginning on page 301. Looking it up, and marking any question that you don't know, will help you remember it. It is also an easy way to record your progress.

1. What is the supreme law of the land?

2. What does the Constitution do?

3. The idea of self-government is in the first three words of the Constitution. What are these words?

4. What is an amendment?

5. What do we call the first ten amendments to the Constitution?

6. What is one right or freedom from the First Amendment?*

7. How many amendments does the Constitution have?

8. What did the Declaration of Independence do?

9. What are two rights in the Declaration of Independence?

10. What is freedom of religion?

* marks the only questions you need to know if you are
over 65 and meet the permanent resident requirements.

11. What is the economic system in the United States? *

12. What is the "rule of law"?

13. Name one branch or part of government.

14. What stops one branch of government from becoming too powerful?

15. Who is in charge of the executive branch?

16. Who makes federal laws?

17. What are the two parts of the U.S. Congress? *

18. How many U.S. Senators are there?

19. We elect a U.S. Senator for how many years?

20. Who is one of your state's U.S. Senators now? *

21. The House of Representatives has how many voting members?

22. We elect a U.S. Representative for how many years?

23. Name your U.S. Representative.

24. Who does a U.S. Senator represent?

25. Why do some states have more Representatives than other states?

26. We elect a President for how many years?

27. In what month do we vote for President? *

28. What is the name of the President of the U.S. now?

29. What is the name of the Vice President of the United States now?

30. If the President can no longer serve, who becomes President?

31. If both the President and the Vice President can no longer serve, who becomes President?

32. Who is the Commander in Chief of the military?

33. Who signs bills to become laws?

34. Who vetoes bills?

35. What does the President's Cabinet do?

36. What are two Cabinet-level positions?

37. What does the judicial branch do?

38. What is the highest court in the United States?

39. How many justices are on the Supreme Court?

40. Who is the Chief Justice of the United States now?

41. Under our Constitution, some powers belong to the federal government. What is one power of the federal government?

42. Under our Constitution, some powers belong to the states. What is one power of the states?

43. Who is the Governor of your state now?

44. What is the capital of your state? *

45. What are the two major political parties in the United States? *

46. What is the political party of the President now?

47. What is the name of the Speaker of the House of Representatives now?

48. There are four amendments to the Constitution about who can vote. Describe one of them.

49. What is one responsibility that is only for United States citizens?*

50. Name one right only for United States citizens.

51. What are two rights of everyone living in the United States?

52. What do we show loyalty to when we say the Pledge of Allegiance?

53. What is one promise you make when you become a United States citizen?

54. How old do citizens have to be to vote for President? *

55. What are two ways that Americans can participate in their democracy?

56. When is the last day you can send in federal income tax forms? *

57. When must all men register for the Selective Service?

58. What is one reason colonists came to America?

59. Who lived in America before the Europeans arrived?

60. What group of people was taken to America and sold as slaves?

61. Why did the colonists fight the British?

62. Who wrote the Declaration of Independence?

63. When was the Declaration of Independence adopted?

64. There were 13 original states. Name three.

65. What happened at the Constitutional Convention?

66. When was the Constitution written?

67. The Federalist Papers supported the passage of the U.S. Constitution. Name one of the writers.

68. What is one thing Benjamin Franklin is famous for?

69. Who is the "Father of Our Country"?

70. Who was the first President? *

71. What territory did the United States buy from France in 1803?

72. Name one war fought by the United States in the 1800s.

73. Name the U.S. war between the North and the South.

74. Name one problem that led to the Civil War.

75. What was one important thing that Abraham Lincoln did?*

76. What did the Emancipation Proclamation do?

77. What did Susan B. Anthony do?

78. Name one war fought by the United States in the 1900s.*

79. Who was President during World War I?

80. Who was President during the Great Depression and World War II?

81. Who did the United States fight in World War II?

82. Before he was President, Eisenhower was a general. What war was he in?

83. During the Cold War, what was the main concern of the United States?

84. What movement tried to end racial discrimination?

85. What did Martin Luther King, Jr. do? *

86. What major event happened on September 11, 2001, in the United States?

87. Name one American Indian tribe in the United States.

88. Name one of the two longest rivers in the United States.

89. What ocean is on the West Coast of the United States?

90. What ocean is on the East Coast of the United States?

91. Name one U.S. territory.

92. Name one state that borders Canada.

93. Name one state that borders Mexico.

94. What is the capital of the United States? *

95. Where is the Statue of Liberty? *

96. Why does the flag have 13 stripes?

97. Why does the flag have 50 stars? *

98. What is the name of the national anthem?

99. When do we celebrate Independence Day?*

100. Name two national U.S. holidays.

Use the space below to write any questions or information that you want to practice

Notes

_____

_____

_____

_____

_____

_____

_____

_____

_____

_____

_____

_____

_____

_____

_____

_____

_____

_____

_____

_____

_____

_____

_____

17

"65/20"
The 20 Civics Questions
for People 65 and Older

Famous Symbols of America

The American Flag

Civics Test Question # 96: Why does the flag have 13 stripes?

Answers: Because there were 13 original colonies

Civics Test Question #97: Why does the flag have 50 stars?

Answers: Because there were 50 original states.

17

65/20
20 Civics Questions

*If you are 65 years old or older and have been a legal permanent resident of the United States for 20 or more years, you can be tested only on the 20 questions below (marked with an asterisk (*) in chapter 16). These 20 questions and answers are listed below and in a multiple choice section that follows. All answers are correct. You only need to know one answer unless the question asks for more.

Questions: #6, 11, 13, 17, 20, 27, 28, 44, 45, 49, 54, 56, 70, 75, 78, 85, 94, 95, 97, 99

6. What is one right or freedom from the First Amendment?*

- speech
- religion
- assembly
- press
- petition the government

11. What is the economic system in the United States?*

- capitalist economy
- market economy

13. Name one branch or part of the government.*

- Congress (or legislative)
- President (or executive)
- the courts (or judicial)

17. What are the two parts of the U.S. Congress?*

the Senate and House (of Representatives)

20. Who is one of your state's U.S. Senators now?*

Answers will be different for each state.

[District of Columbia residents and residents of U.S. territories should answer that D.C. (or the territory where the applicant lives) has no U.S. Senators.]

27. In what month do we vote for President?*

November

28. What is the name of the President of the United States now?*

- Barack Obama
- Obama

44. What is the capital of your state?*

Answers will be different by state. See page 233.

[District of Columbia residents should answer that D.C. is not a state and does not have a capital. Residents of U.S. territories should name the capital of the territory.]

45. What are the two major political parties in the United States?*

    Democratic and Republican

49. What is one responsibility that is only for United States citizens?*

    - serve on a jury
    - vote in a federal election

54. How old do citizens have to be to vote for President?*

    eighteen (18) and older

56. When is the last day you can send in federal income tax forms?*

    April 15

70.   Who was the first President?*

    (George) Washington

75. What was one important thing that Abraham Lincoln did?*

    - freed the slaves (Emancipation Proclamation)
    - saved (or preserved) the Union
    - led the United States during the Civil War

78. Name one war fought by the United States in the 1900s.*

- World War I
- World War II
- Korean War
- Vietnam War
- (Persian) Gulf War

85. What did Martin Luther King, Jr. do?*

- fought for civil rights
- worked for equality for all Americans

94. What is the capital of the United States?*

Washington, D.C.

95. Where is the Statue of Liberty?*

- New York (Harbor)
- Liberty Island

[Also acceptable are New Jersey, near New York City, and on the Hudson (River).]

97. Why does the flag have 50 stars?*

- because there is one star for each state
- because each star represents a state
- because there are 50 states

99. When do we celebrate Independence Day?*

July 4

65/20
Multiple Choice Civics Questions
Practice for People Over 65

Reminder: At your citizenship interview, the civics questions will not be multiple choice. But this is a good way to practice.

Directions: Read each civics question below, and circle the letter of the correct answer.

1. What is one branch of the U.S. government?

a. Senate
b. House of Representatives
c. The Supreme Court
d. Executive

2. What is the economic system of the United States?

a. socialist
b. capitalist
c. democratic
d. communist

3. When is the last day you can send in federal income tax forms?

a. July 4
b. March 15
c. April 15
d. May 15

4. What is one responsibility of a U.S. citizen?

a. get a passport
b. get a driver's license
c. all of these
d. serve on a jury

Answers: 1 d, 2 b, 3 c, 4 d

5. What is one right or freedom from the First Amendment?

a. voting
b. the right to employment
c. a jury trial
d. speech

6. What are the two political parties of the United States now?

a. Republican and the Whig Parties
b. Democratic - Republican Party and the Progressive Parties
c. Socialist Party and Green Parties
d. Republican and Democratic Parties

7. Name one war fought by the U.S. in the 1800s.

a. World War II
b. Civil War
c. Korean War
d. World War I

8. What is the name of the U.S. President now?

a. George W. Bush
b. George Washington
c. Barack Obama
d. Bill Clinton

9. What are the two parts of the U.S. Congress?

a. the Senate and House of Representatives
b. the House of Representatives and the courts
c. the House of Lords and the House of Commons
d. the Senate and the courts

Answers: 5 d, 6 d, 7 b, 8 c, 9 a

10. Who was the first president of the United States?

a. George Washington
b. Abraham Lincoln
c. George W. Bush
d. Thomas Jefferson

11. What was an important thing that Abraham Lincoln did?

a. wrote the Declaration of Independence
b. led U.S. in World War I
c. freed all the slaves
d. served in the Continental Congress

12. What did Martin Luther King, Jr. do?

a. freed the slaves
b. wrote the Declaration of Independence
c. fought for civil rights
d. led the U.S. in World War I

13. Name one state that borders Canada.

a. Oregon
b. South Dakota
c. Rhode Island
d. Maine

14. What is the capital of the United States?

a. Philadelphia
b. New York City
c. Los Angeles
d. Washington, D.C.

Answers: 10 a, 11 c, 12 c, 13 d, 14 d

15. Why does the flag have 50 stars?

a. for the 50 original colonies
b. for the 50 American presidents
c. for the 50 states
d. for the 50 Articles of Confederation

16. When do we celebrate Independence Day?

a. April 15
b. January 1
c. July 14
d. July 4

17. Where is the Statue of Liberty?

a. the Pacific Ocean
b. Washington, D.C.
c. Las Vegas
d. New York harbor

18. How old do citizens have to be to vote for President?

a. eighteen (18) and older
b. sixteen (16) and older
c. twenty-one (21) and older
d. twenty (20) and older

Answers: 15 c, 16 d, 17 d, 18 a

19. Name one war fought in the 1900s.

a. the American Revolution
b. World War I
c. the Civil War
d. the Spanish-American War

20. What is one right or freedom in the First Amendment?

a. freedom to travel
b. the right to serve on a jury
c. the right to carry a gun
d. freedom of religion

Answers: 19 b, 20 d

Your Score _____/ 25

Also know:

Who is one of your state's two U.S. senators?

_____

What is your state capital?

_____

A Tip!

*Look up any answers that you missed on the list of Civics Test questions and answers, or on the flashcards. Then mark that question so you remember to review it.

Read the multiple choice question and the correct answer out loud to help remember it and to practice your reading in English. Sometimes the USCIS officer will ask you to read a sentence for the reading test that includes civics vocabulary. Reading out loud will help.

65/20 Flashcards: The civics flashcards for people 65+ are in the "100 civics questions" flashcard section. They are the 20 questions listed and marked with an *.

"65/20" Civics Questions Only—For Easier Review

*If you are 65 years old or older and have been a legal permanent resident of the United States for 20 or more years, you only need to know the questions that have been marked with an asterisk.(*) They are also listed below.

Check your answers in Chapter 15, p.251

Questions: #6, 11, 13, 17, 20, 27, 28, 44, 45, 49, 54, 56, 70, 75, 78, 85, 94, 95, 97, 99

6. What is one right or freedom from the First Amendment? *

11. What is the economic system in the United States? *

13. Name one branch or part of the government.*

17. What are the two parts of the U.S. Congress? *

20. Who is one of your state's U.S. Senators now? *

27. In what month do we vote for President? *

28. What is the name of the President of the United States now? *

44. What is the capital of your state? *

45. What are the two major political parties in the United States? *

49. What is one responsibility that is only for United States citizens? *

54. How old do citizens have to be to vote for President? *

56. When is the last day you can send in federal income tax forms? *

70. Who was the first President? *

75. What was one important thing that Abraham Lincoln did? *

78. Name one war fought by the United States in the 1900s.*

85. What did Martin Luther King, Jr. do? *

94. What is the capital of the United States? *

95. Where is the Statue of Liberty? *

97. Why does the flag have 50 stars? *

99. When do we celebrate Independence Day? *

Chapter 18

Civics Flashcards

Practice the Civics Questions with
Flashcards

American Political Parties

Republicans   Democrats

Civics Test Question #45: What are the two major political parties in the United States?

Answer: The Democratic Party and the Republican Party

100 Civics Questions
Flash Card Practice

Make Your Own Flashcards

Directions:

1. Remove the next pages from this book.

2. Cut each page on the dotted lines

------------------------- so that you have three
separate cards per page.

3. Keep the cut papers ("flashcards") in an envelope.

4. Practice. Read the question on the front and give
the answer. Then look at the back to see if your
answer was correct.

front	back
	The Constitution

5. Keep the questions that you missed in a separate
group from the questions that you already know the
answers to. Practice the ones you don't know again
and again.

65/20

The 20 flashcards with civics questions for people who are 65+ and have been permanent residents for 20 years are marked with an *. They are:

Questions: #6, 11, 13, 17, 20, 27, 28, 44, 45, 49, 54, 56, 70, 75, 78, 85, 94, 95, 97, 99

1. What is the supreme (highest) law of the land?

cut here—>- - - - - - - - - - - - - - - - - - -

2. What does the Constitution do?

cut here—>- - - - - - - - - - - - - - - - - - -

3. The idea of self-government is in the first three words of the Constitution.
    What are these words?

1. the Constitution

2. sets up the government

You need to know one answer.
For more choices, see page 225.

3. We the People

4. What is an amendment?

----

5. What do we call the first ten amendments to the Constitution?

----

6. What is one right or freedom from the First Amendment?*

4. a change (to the Constitution)

5. the Bill of Rights

6. freedom of religion

You need to know one.

For more choices, see page 226.

7. How many amendments does the Constitution have?

- -

8. What did the Declaration of Independence do?

- -

9. What are two rights in the Declaration of Independence?

7. Twenty-seven (27)

8. announced our independence (from Great Britain)

You need to know one answer.
For more choices, see page 226.

9. –life
–liberty

You need to know two rights.
For more choices, see page 226.

10. What is freedom of religion?

- -

11. What is the economic system in the United States?*

- -

12. What is the "rule of law"?

10. People can observe (have) any religion or no religion

11. capitalist economy

12. Everyone must follow the law.

You need to know one answer.
For other choices, see page 227.

13. Name one branch or part of the government.*

----

14. What stops one branch of government from becoming too powerful?

----

15. Who is in charge of the executive branch?

13. Congress

You need to know one branch.
For other choices, see page 227.

14. checks and balances

15. the President

16. Who makes federal laws?

----

17. What are the two parts of
    the U.S. Congress?*

----

18. How many U.S. Senators
    are there?

16. Congress

17. the Senate and House (of Representatives)

18. one hundred (100)

19. We elect a U.S. Senator for how many years?

- -

20. Who is one of your state's U.S. Senators now?*

- -

21. The House of Representatives has how many voting members?

19. six (6)

20. Answers will differ.

[District of Columbia residents and residents of U.S. territories should answer that D.C. (or the territory where the applicant lives) has no U.S. Senators.] Find your senator at www.senate.gov.

21. four hundred thirty-five (435)

22. We elect a U.S. Representative for how many years?

----

23. Name your U.S. Representative.

----

24. Who does a U.S. Senator represent?

22. two (2)

23. *Answers will be different for every state.

If you live in a U.S. territory with non-voting Delegates or Resident Commissioners you can say that person's name. Also acceptable is any statement that the territory has no (voting) Representatives in Congress. Everyone else can find the representative at www.house.gov.

24. All the people.

25. Why do some states have
    more Representatives than
    other states?

----

26. We elect a President for
    how many years?

----

27. In what month do we vote
    for President?*

25. (because) they have more people

You need to know one answer.
For other choices, see page 229.

26. four (4)

27. November

28. What is the name of the President of the United States now?*

- -

29. What is the name of the Vice President of the United States now?

- -

30. If the President can no longer serve, who becomes President?

28. Barack Obama

For other ways to say this,
see page 230.

29. Joe Biden

For other ways to say this,
see page 230.

30. the Vice President

31. If both the President and the Vice President can no longer serve, who becomes President?

- -

32. Who is the Commander in Chief of the military?

- -

33. Who signs bills to become laws?

31. the Speaker of the House

32. the President

33. the President

34. Who vetoes bills?

----

35. What does the President's
     Cabinet do?

----

36. What are two Cabinet-level
     positions?

34. the President

35. advises the President

36. Vice President;
     Secretary of State

You only need to know 2 positions.
For other choices, see page 231.

37. What does the judicial
    branch do?

----

38. What is the highest court in
    the United States?

----

39. How many justices are on
    the Supreme Court?

37. explains laws

You need to know one answer.
For other choices, see page 232.

38. the Supreme Court

39. nine (9)

40. Who is the Chief Justice of the United States now?

- -

41. Under our Constitution, some powers belong to the federal government. What is one power of the federal government?

- -

42. Under our Constitution, some powers belong to the states. What is one power of the states?

40. John Roberts

41. to declare war

You need to know one power.
For other choices, see page 232.

42. to give a driver's license

You only need to know one power.
For more choices, see page 233.

43. Who is the Governor of your state now?

- -

44. What is the capital of your state?*

- -

45. What are the two major political parties in the United States?*

43. Answers will differ.

[District of Columbia residents should answer that D.C. does not have a Governor.]

44. Answers will differ—
see page 233.

[District of Columbia residents should answer that D.C. is not a state and does not have a capital. Residents of U.S. territories should name the capital of the territory.]

45. Democratic and Republican

46. What is the political party
of the President now?

- -

47. What is the name of the
Speaker of the House of
Representatives?

- -

48. There are four amendments
to the Constitution about
who can vote.
Describe one of them.

46. Democratic (Party)

47. (John) Boehner

48. Any U.S. citizen over 18
years old can vote.

You need to know one amendment.
For other choices, see page 235.

49. What is one responsibility
     that is only for United
     States citizens?*

- -

50. Name one right only for
     United States citizens.

- -

51. What are two rights of
     everyone living in the United
     States?

49. to serve on a jury

You only need to know one answer.
For other choices, see page 235.

50. to vote in a federal election

51. freedom of religion

You need to know one right.
For more choices, see page 235.

52. What do we show loyalty to when we say the Pledge of Allegiance?

- -

53. What is one promise you make when you become a United States citizen?

- -

54. How old do citizens have to be to vote for President?

52. the United States

53. to defend the U.S.

You need to know one answer.
For more choices, see page 236.

54. 18 (eighteen and older)

55. What are two ways that Americans can participate in their democracy?

----

56. When is the last day you can send in federal income tax forms?*

----

57. When must all men register for the Selective Service?

55. (1) vote;
     (2) join a political party

For more choices of answers, see page 236.

56. April 15

57. at age eighteen (18)

58. What is one reason colonists came to America?

----

59. Who lived in America before the Europeans arrived?

----

60. What group of people was taken to America and sold as slaves?

58. freedom

You need to know one reason.
For more reasons, see page 237.

59. American Indians

For another way to say it, see
page 237.

60. people from Africa

61. Why did the colonists fight the British? (1 reason)

- -

62. Who wrote the Declaration of Independence?

- -

63. When was the Declaration of Independence adopted?

61. because of high taxes
("taxation without representation")

You need to know one answer.
For other choices, see page 238.

62. (Thomas) Jefferson

63. July 4, 1776

64. There were 13 original states. Name three.

----

65. What happened at the Constitutional Convention?

----

66. When was the Constitution written?

64. New York
    New Jersey
    North Carolina

For a complete list, see page 238.

65. The Constitution was written.

For other answers, see page 239.

66. 1787

67. The Federalist Papers supported the passage of the U.S. Constitution. Name one of the writers.

---

68. What is one thing Benjamin Franklin is famous for?

---

69. Who is the "Father of Our Country"?

67. (James) Madison

You need to know one writer.
For other choices, see page 239.

68. started the first free libraries

You need to know one answer.
For more choices, see page 239.

69. (George) Washington

70. Who was the first President?*

- -

71. What territory did the United States buy from France in 1803?

- -

72. Name one war fought by the United States in the 1800s.

70. (George) Washington

71. Louisiana

For another way to say this,
see page 240.

72. Civil War

You need to know one war.
For more choices, see page 240.

73. Name the U.S. war between the North and the South.

----

74. Name one problem that led to the Civil War.

----

75. What was one important thing that Abraham Lincoln did?*

73. the Civil War

For another way to say this,
see page 241.

74. slavery

You need to know one answer.
For other choices, see page 241.

75. freed the slaves

You need to know one answer.
For more choices, see page 241.

76. What did the Emancipation Proclamation do?

----

77. What did Susan B. Anthony do?

----

78. Name one war fought by the United States in the 1900s.*

76. freed the slaves

You need to know one answer. For another choice, see page 242.

77. fought for women's rights

You need to know one answer. For more choices, see page 242.

78. World War I

You need to know one answer. For more choices, see page 242.

79. Who was President during World War I?

----

80. Who was President during the Great Depression and World War II?

----

81. Who did the United States fight in World War II?

79. (Woodrow) Wilson

80. (Franklin) Roosevelt

81. Japan, Germany, and Italy

82. Before he was President, Eisenhower was a general. What war was he in?

---

83. During the Cold War, what was the main concern of the United States?

---

84. What movement tried to end racial discrimination?

82. World War II

83. Communism

84. the civil rights movement

85. What did Martin Luther King, Jr. do?*

----

86. What major event happened on September 11, 2001, in the United States?

----

87. Name one American Indian tribe in the United States.
   - the Crow
   [A longer list is on page 244.]

85. He worked for equality for all Americans

You need to know one answer.
For other ways to answer, see page 243.

86. Terrorists attacked the United States.

87. Pueblo

You need to know one tribe.
For more tribes, see page 244.

88. Name one of the two longest rivers in the United States.

---

89. What ocean is on the West Coast of the United States?

---

90. What ocean is on the East Coast of the United States?

88. Missouri (River)

You need to know one river.
For the other river, see page 244.

89. Pacific (Ocean)

90. Atlantic (Ocean)

91.   Name one U.S. territory.

- -

92.   Name one state that
      borders Canada.

- -

93.   Name one state that
      borders Mexico.

91. Puerto Rico

You need to know one territory.
To see the complete list, see page 245.

92. Alaska

You need to know one state.
To see the complete list, see page 245.

93. California

You need to know one state.
To see a complete list, see page 245.

94. What is the capital of the United States?*

----

95. Where is the Statue of Liberty?*

----

96. Why does the flag have 13 stripes?

94. Washington, D.C.

95. New York (Harbor)

You need to know one answer.
For other ways to answer, see page 246.

96. because there were 13 original colonies

You need to know one answer.
For more choices, see page 246.

97. Why does the flag have 50 stars?*

- -

98. What is the name of the national anthem?

- -

99. When do we celebrate Independence Day?*

97. because there are 50 states

You need to know one answer.
For other ways to say this, see page 246.

98. "The Star-Spangled Banner"

99. July 4

100. Name two national U.S. holidays.

- -

100. -Thanksgiving
- Christmas

You need to know two holidays.
For the complete list, see page 247.

Appendix

Deferred Action for Childhood Arrivals
How to Qualify
How to Apply

Appendix

"Deferred Action for Childhood Arrivals"
How to Qualify, How to Apply,
Questions and Answers

Part I: Your Deferred Action Checklist

"Do I Qualify for 'Deferred Action for Childhood Arrivals?"

Below is a checklist to help make all of the USCIS steps clear. You must check ALL 7 of these to qualify. You can request "Deferred Action for Childhood Arrivals" if you:

__1. Were under the age of 31 as of June 15, 2012;   AND

__2. Came to the U.S. before your 16th birthday;   AND

__3. Have continuously lived in the United States from June 15, 2007 to the present time;   AND

__4. Were physically present in the United States on June 15, 2012, AND when you applied to USCIS for Deferred Action for Childhood Arrivals; AND

__5. Entered the U.S. without permission ("without inspection") before June 15, 2012, OR your legal immigration status was expired before June 15, 2012;

                                AND

__6. Are currently in school, OR have a high school diploma (or equivalent, like the GED certificate), OR are an honorably discharged veteran of the Coast Guard or Armed Forces of the United States;

                                AND

__7. Have not been convicted of a felony, significant misdemeanor, three or more other misdemeanors, and do not otherwise pose a threat to national security or public safety.

What Kind of Documents Do I Need to Show I Qualify?

The chart below shows examples of documents you can use to qualify for consideration of deferred action. Please see the instructions on Form I-821D, "Consideration of Deferred Action for Childhood Arrivals", for more examples and information.

Examples of Documents to Submit to Show USCIS that you Meet the Guidelines

Proof of identity	• Passport • Birth certificate with photo identification • School or military ID with photo • Any U.S. government immigration or other document bearing your name and photo
Proof you came to U.S. before your 16th birthday	• Passport with admission stamp • Form I-94/I-95/I-94W • School records from the U.S. schools you have attended • Any Immigration and Naturalization Service or DHS document stating your date of entry (Form I-862, Notice to Appear) • Travel records • Hospital or medical records
Proof of immigration status	• Form I-94/I-95/I-94W with authorized stay expiration date • Final order of exclusion, deportation, or removal issued as of June 15, 2012 • A charging document placing you into removal proceedings
Proof of Presence in U.S. on June 15, 2012	• Rent receipts or utility bills • Employment records (pay stubs, W-2 Forms, etc) • School records (letters, report cards,) • Military records (Form DD-214 or NGB Form 22)

Examples of Documents to Submit to Show USCIS that you Meet the Guidelines

Proof you lived continuously in the U.S. since June 15, 2007

- Official records from a religious entity confirming participation in a religious ceremony
- Copies of money order receipts for money sent in or out of the country
- Passport entries
- Birth certificates of children born in the U.S.
- Dated bank transactions
- Social Security card
- Automobile license receipts or registration
- Deeds, mortgages, rental agreement contracts
- Tax receipts, insurance policies

Students:

Proof that you were a student when you applied for Deferred Action for Childhood Arrivals

- School records (transcripts, report cards, etc) from the school that you are currently attending in the United States showing the name(s) of the school(s) and periods of school attendance and the current educational or grade level
- U.S. high school diploma or certificate of completion
- U.S. GED certificate

Veterans:

Proof you are an honorably discharged veteran of the U.S. Armed Forces or the U.S. Coast Guard

- Form DD-214, Certificate of Release or Discharge from Active Duty
- NGB Form 22, National Guard Report of Separation and Record of Service
- Military personnel records
- Military health records

Important Information

USCIS forms:

Consideration of Deferred Action for Childhood Arrivals --
Form I-821D

Application for Employment Authorization –
Form I-765 Worksheet -- Form I-765WS

E-Notification of Application/Petition Acceptance –
Form G-1145

USCIS web sites:

Information about "Deferred Action for Childhood Arrivals" process and frequently asked questions –
www.uscis.gov/childhoodarrivals

Consideration of Deferred Action for Childhood Arrivals Form I-821D—
www.uscis.gov/I-821D

E-Notification of Application/Petition Acceptance Form—
www.uscis.gov/G-1145

USCIS Notice to AppearPolicy—
www.uscis.gov/NTA

For More Information:

General Information – www.usa.gov
New Immigrants – www.welcometoUSA.gov
U.S. Immigration & Customs Enforcement – www.ice.gov

II. Applying

To Apply, you must:

___ **1. Collect documents** to show that they qualify

___ **2. Complete application forms:**

- Form I-821D ("Consideration of Deferred Action for Childhood Arrivals")

- Form I-765, ("Application for Employment Authorization");

- Form I-765WS, Form I-765 Worksheet.

___ **3. Include a check or money order** payable to Department of Homeland Security. Cost: $465.

III. Fee Exemption

Fee Exemption "Do I have to pay?"

Form I-765 costs $380 plus $85 for biometrics (fingerprints). There is no charge for Form I-821D. All three forms must be submitted with your payment or your USCIS approval of fee exemption to the nearest USCIS Lockbox (see below).

Requirements for a Fee Exemption. To qualify for a fee exemption you need to submit a letter and documents showing 2 things:

(1) Income Problem. Your income is less than 150% of the U.S. poverty level ($16,755 for a single person*) . USCIS has a chart that lists these rates. Here is an example for 2012:

150% of Poverty Level in 2012 (from USCIS):

- $16,755   for a 1 person household

- $22,695   for a 2 person household

- $28,635   for a 3 person household

- $34,575   for a 4 person household

*These are the rates for all 48 contiguous states, but do not include Alaska and Hawaii. In those two states, "150% of poverty level" can be several thousands of dollars higher.

For information for larger households, see the complete chart at: `http://www.uscis.gov/files/form/i-912p.pdf`. You can check this USCIS website each year for updates.

AND, you also need....

(2) Financial problems. You also need to have one of the following financial problems:

- You are under 18 years old and do not have financial support from your pare4nts or other family. This includes if you are homeless or in foster care, OR

- You have a serious chronic disability and cannot care for yourself, OR

- You owe at least $25,000 (within a year before you applied for Deferred Action) because of medical expenses for yourself or an immediate family member.

AND

(3) Send a Letter. If you have both of these problems, you may qualify for a fee exemption. You need to send a letter (in English) requesting an exemption for the "Deferred Action for Childhood Arrivals" fee. Include your name, and the reason that you are asking for an exemption in your letter.

You can write one of the following sentences in your letter as your reason for requesting an exemption:

1. "I am under 18 and do not have financial support from my parents. My income is less than (fill in amount) ."

2. "I am under 18 and I am homeless. My income is less than $ (fill in the amount)".

3. "I am disabled and cannot take care of myself. My income is less than $ (fill in the amount). "

4. "I owe $25,000 (or more) for medical expenses in the last year. My income is less than $ (fill in amount)."

Include copies of documents that show these things are true. These documents must be in English or with a certified translation.

For evidence that you need a fee exemption, USCIS will accept:

- affidavits from community-based or religious organizations to establish your homelessness or lack of parental or other familial financial support.

- copies of tax returns, banks statement, pay stubs, or other reliable evidence of income level. Evidence can also include an affidavit from the applicant or a responsible third party attesting that the applicant does not file tax returns, has no bank accounts, and/or has no income to prove income level.

- copies of medical records, insurance records, bank state-ments, or other reliable evidence of unreimbursed medical expenses of at least $25,000.

__Be sure to sign your letter! Be sure to include copies of documents showing your financial problems.

__Mail your request for fee exemption to:

U.S. Citizenship and Immigration Services
Attn: Deferred Action for Childhood Arrivals
Fee
Exemption Request
P.O. Box 75036
Washington, DC 20013

Remember: Do not file your forms for "Deferred Action on Childhood Arrivals" until USCIS approves or denies your fee exemption.

III. If you are approved for an exemption...Make a copy of the USCIS letter approving your fee exemption. Attach that to the front of your Deferred Action forms and mail it to the nearest USCIS Lockbox.

IV. If you are not approved for an exemption...send your Deferred Action forms to USCIS and include your $465.

Review: Sending Your Application

1. __ Complete and Sign 3 Application Forms:

- Form I-821D ("Consideration of Deferred Action for Childhood Arrivals")

- Form I-765, ("Application for Employment Authorization");

- Form I-765WS, Form I-765 Worksheet.

2. __ Include copies of documents that show you qualify.

3. __Mail everything to the USCIS Lockbox (see next page for the address nearest you):

(1) the 3 required forms, completed and signed;

(2) documents to prove you qualify; and

(3) $465 payment payable to the Department of Homeland Security (DHS) or a copy of the exemption letter you received from USCIS.

4. __Biometrics Appointment. USCIS will send you a letter telling you when and where to go for your biometrics (fingerprinting) appointment. It will be at your local USCIS Application Support Center.

5. __Are you approved for "Consideration for Deferred Action for Childhood Arrivals"? You can check online to see if your application is accepted at:

www.uscis.gov/childhoodarrivals

USCIS Lockbox: Mail to Direct Filing Addresses for Consideration of Deferred Action for Childhood Arrivals

I live in ...	U.S.Postal Service	USPS Express Mail/Courier
Arizona, California	**USCIS Phoenix Lockbox Facility** USCIS P.O. Box20700 Phoenix, AZ 85036-0700	**USCIS Phoenix Lockbox Facility** USCIS Attn: DACA 1820 E. Skyharbor Circle S Suite 100 Phoenix, AZ 85034
Alaska, Alabama, Arkansas, Florida, Guam, Hawaii, Idaho, Iowa,Kansas, Louisiana,Minnesota, Missouri, Mississippi, Montana, North Dakota,Nebraska, New Mexico,Oklahoma, Puerto Rico,Saipan,South Dakota,Tennessee, Texas, Utah, U.S. Virgin Islands,or Wyoming.	**USCIS Dallas Lockbox Facility** USCIS P.O. Box 660045 Dallas, TX 75266-0045	**USCIS Dallas Lockbox Facility** USCIS ATTN: DACA 2501 S. State Hwy.121, Business Suite 400 Lewisville, TX 75067

I live in...	USCIS Chicago Lockbox Facility	USCIS Chicago Lockbox Facility
Colorado, Connecticut, Delaware, District of Columbia, Georgia, Illinois, Indiana, Kentucky, Massachusetts, Maryland, Maine, Michigan, Nevada, North Carolina, New Hampshire, New Jersey, New York, Ohio, Oregon, Pennsylvania, Rhode Island, South Carolina, Virginia, Vermont, Washington, Wisconsin, or West Virginia.	USCIS P.O. Box 5757 Chicago, IL 60680-5757	USCIS Attn: DACA 131 S. Dearborn – 3rd Floor Chicago, IL 60603-5517

For Questions About Filing.

If you have questions about filing, go to the USCIS website at `www.uscis.gov/I-821D` or contact the USCIS National Customer Service at: 1-800-375-5283.

Questions and answers about this program begin on the next page.

[The following section includes from *How Do I...Request Consideration of Deferred Action for Childhood Arrivals?* Be sure to check with the USCIS website for any changes.]

Questions and Answers

1. Will USCIS tell me when my form has been accepted?

Yes. They try to respond in 90 days. If you include **Form G-1145, "E-Notification of Application/Petition Acceptance"** with your forms and check, you can receive an e-mail or text message telling you that your request was accepted. Please see www.uscis.gov/G-1145 for E-notification instructions.

2. What does "biometrics" mean and how do I get it done?

Biometrics means having your fingerprints taken. USCIS will use them to check your background and check any criminal record.

Please Note: You will submit your forms, money and documents and then you will receive a receipt from USCIS If your application was accepted, USCIS will also ask you to go to an Application Support Center (ASC) for biometric services. Please make sure you read and follow the directions in the notice. If you do not go to this appointment, your Deferred Action request may be denied.

3. If USCIS does not exercise deferred action in my case, will I be deported?

If your case does not involve a criminal offense, fraud, or a threat to national security or public safety, it will not be referred to ICE for deportation except in exceptional circumstances. For more detailed information on the applicable NTA policy visit **www.uscis.gov/NTA.**

4. If my case is deferred, will I be eligible for premium tax credits and reduced cost sharing through the Affordable Insurance Exchange starting in 2014?

No.

5. Will my information be used to deport any of my family?

No. Information provided in this request is protected.

6. Does this process apply to me if I am currently in removal proceedings (being deported), have a final removal order, or have a voluntary departure order?

Yes, if you are currently in immigration detention and believe you meet the guidelines you can request Deferred Action—but do <u>not</u> ask USCIS.

You should identify yourself to your detention officer or contact the ICE Office of the Public Advocate through the Office's hotline at 1-888-351-4024 (staffed 9 a.m. – 5 p.m., Monday – Friday) or by email at `EROPublicAdvocate@ice.dhs.gov`.

7. Does deferred action provide me with a path to permanent residence status or citizenship?

No. Only the Congress can decide the requirements for permanent residence and citizenship.

8. Do I need to be "currently in school" on the date I file my papers?

Yes. You must be enrolled in school on the date you submit a request for consideration of deferred action under this process.

9. Who is "currently in school" under the USCIS guidelines?

To be considered "currently in school" under the guidelines, you must be enrolled in:

- a public or private K-12 school; OR

- a program (including literacy programs and vocational training) that will lead to college education, or job training, or

- a program to help you get a high school diploma or its legal equivalen (including a certificate of completion, certificate of attendance, or alternate award), or in passing an exam, like the General Educational Development (GED) exam.

These programs should get government funding or have a long-term record of success, such as programs at community colleges, and certain long-term community-based organizations.

10. How do I prove that I am currently in school?

You need to show USCIS proof that you are enrolled. This includes:

- acceptance letters,
- school registration cards,
- letters from school or program,
- transcripts,
- report cards, or
- progress reports

Documents should show the name of the school or program, date of enrollment, and current educational or grade level, if relevant.

11. If I am enrolled in an English as a Second Language (ESL) program, can I meet the guidelines?

Yes, if you are enrolled in an ESL program to help you go to college or get a job. You need a letter from the school saying that college or a job is your goal and that this ESL program has shown to help students do this.

12. If I get approved now because I am in school and I want USCIS to renew my deferral after two years, what will I need to show them?

To get an extension, you will need to show

(1) You are in a K-12 school, you in a program to help you graduate from high school; you are graduating from high school, or,

(2) you have received your GED or other high school diploma equivalent or,

(3) you are enrolled in college, have a job that you trained for, or are making progress toward completing those college or employment goals.

13. May I travel outside of the United States before USCIS has determined whether to defer action in my case?

No. After August 15, 2012, if you travel outside of the United States, you will not be considered for deferred action under this process. If USCIS defers action in your case, you will be permitted to travel outside of the United States only if you apply for and receive advance parole from USCIS.

Any travel outside of the United States that occurred before August 15, 2012, will be assessed by USCIS to determine whether the travel qualifies as "brief, casual and innocent".

14. Will USCIS do a background check when reviewing my request for consideration of deferred action for childhood arrivals?

Yes. If you have been convicted of any felony, a significant misdemeanor offense, three or more misdemeanor offenses or otherwise pose a threat to national security or public safety, your request will be denied.

15. If USCIS does not approve deferred action for me, will I be placed in removal proceedings?

No, in most cases. If your case does not involve a criminal offense, fraud, or a threat to national security or public safety, your case will not be placed in removal proceedings.

16. Can I appeal USCIS's decision?

No. You cannot file a motion to reopen or reconsider, and cannot appeal the decision if USCIS denies your request for consideration of deferred action for childhood arrivals. USCIS will not review its discretionary determinations.

However, you can ask for a review using the Service Request Management Tool (SRMT) process if you met all of the process guidelines and you believe that your request was denied due to one of the following errors:

- USCIS denied the request for consideration of deferred action for childhood arrivals based on abandonment and you claim that you did respond to a Request for Evidence within the prescribed time; or

- USCIS mailed the Request for Evidence to the wrong address, even though you had submitted a Form AR-11, Change of Address, or changed your address online at www.uscis.gov before the issuance of the Request for Evidence.

17. Can I extend the period of deferred action in my case?

Yes. As long as you were not above the age of 30 on June 15, 2012, you may request a renewal after turning 31. Your request for an extension will be considered on a case-by-case basis.

18. If my period of deferred action is extended, will I need to re-apply for an extension of my employment authorization?

Yes. If USCIS decides to defer action for additional periods beyond the initial two years, you must also have requested an extension of your employment authorization.

19. Will USCIS personnel responsible for reviewing requests for an exercise of prosecutorial discretion under this process receive special training?

Yes. USCIS personnel responsible for considering requests for consideration of deferred action for childhood arrivals will receive special training.

20. What should I do if I meet the guidelines of this process and have been issued an ICE detainer following an arrest by a state or local law enforcement officer?

If you meet the guidelines and have been served a detainer, you should immediately contact either the Law Enforcement Support Center's hotline at 1-855-448-6903 (staffed 24 hours a day, 7 days a week) or the ICE Office of the Public Advocate either through the Office's hotline at 1-888-351-4024 (staffed 9 a.m. – 5 p.m., Monday – Friday) or by email at EROPublicAdvocate@ice.dhs.gov.

Avoiding Scams and Preventing Fraud

21. Someone told me if I pay them a fee, they can get my Deferred Action for Childhood Arrivals request approved faster. Is this true?

No. There is no way for someone to get your papers approved faster. Dishonest people may ask you to pay them extra for faster service but that is not possible with USCIS. Documents are received and processed in order. People who ask to be paid to have your papers approved faster are trying to scam you and take your money. Visit USCIS *Avoid Scams* page to learn how you can protect yourself from immigration scams.

Remember: Always make your requests and pay your fees to official government sources like USCIS or the Department of Homeland Security. If you need a lawyer, go to USCIS *Find Legal Services* page to learn how to choose a lawyer or accredited representative.

22. What steps will USCIS and ICE take if someone lies in order to qualify for Deferred Action?

If someone intentionally misrepresents or hides facts to get Deferred Action or a job, they have committed fraud. They will be punished as much as the law allows, including possible criminal prosecution and deportation from the United States.

USCIS in Their Own Words:

To request "Consideration of Deferred Action for Childhood Arrivals" from USCIS, you must submit **Form I-821D, Consideration of Deferred Action for Childhood Arrivals to USCIS**. This form must be completed, properly signed and accompanied by a **Form I-765, Application for Employment Authorization**, and a **Form I-765WS** Worksheet, establishing your economic need for employment. If you fail to submit a completed Form I-765 (along with the accompanying filing fees for that form, totaling $465), USCIS will not consider your request for deferred action. Please read the form instructions to ensure that you submit all the required documentation to support your request.

Failure to submit a completed Form I-765 (along with the accompanying filing fees for that form), will preclude consideration for deferred action. While there is no filing fee for Form I-821D, you must submit the $380 filing fee for Form I-765, which includes the Form I-765WS, and a biometric services fee of $85 required for the Application for Employment Authorization for a total of $465. Please read the form instructions to ensure that you submit all the required documentation to support your request.

You must file your request for consideration of deferred action for childhood arrivals at the USCIS Lockbox. You can find the mailing address and instructions on www.uscis.gov/i-821d. After your Form I-821D, Form I-765, and Form I-765 Worksheet have been received, USCIS will review them for completeness, including submission of the required fee, initial evidence and supporting documents.

If it your request is complete, USCIS will send you a receipt notice. USCIS will then send you an appointment notice to visit an Application Support Center (ASC) for biometric services. Please make sure you read and follow the directions in the notice. Failure to attend your biometrics appointment may delay processing of your request for consideration of deferred action, or may result in a denial of your request.

You may also choose to receive an email and/or text message notifying you that your form has been accepted by completing a **Form G-1145, E-Notification of Application/ Petition Acceptance.**

Each request for consideration of deferred action for childhood arrivals will be reviewed on an individual, case-by-case basis. USCIS may request more information or evidence from you, or request that you appear at a USCIS office. USCIS will notify you of its decision in writing.

Note: All individuals who believe they meet the guidelines, including those in removal proceedings, with a final removal order, or with a voluntary departure order (and not in immigration detention), may affirmatively request consideration of deferred action for childhood arrivals from USCIS through this process.

Individuals who are currently in immigration detention and believe they meet the guide-lines may not request consideration of deferred action from USCIS but may identify themselves to their detention officer or to the ICE Office of the Public Advocate through the Office's hotline at 1-888-351-4024 (staffed 9 a.m. – 5 p.m., Monday – Friday) or by email at **EROPublicAdvocate@ice.dhs.gov**.

Index

address change, 55-56
application to preserve residence (N-470), 41, 43
adjustment of status, 35
books, recommended, 10-11
    bilingual, 10-11
changing status, 35-36
citizenship,
    bars to, 53-54
    permanent, 53
    temporary, 54
citizenship, checklist, 17-18, 57-60, 108
citizenship oath, see *Oath of Allegiance*
citizenship rights, 47
citizenship test,
    checklist, 108
    exemptions, exceptions, modifications, 79-86,
    four parts, 70-74, 75, 97, 99-100, 108
    interview questions, 112-144
    passing scores, 75-76, 99-100, 108
    retaking, 100
civics test, 55, 73-74, 225-370
    exemptions, 81-82
    flashcards, 301-370
    interpreter, 81
    multiple choice questions 251-270, 291-295 ("65/20")
    passing score, 70-72, 75-76, 99-100
    questions for people over 65 (65/20), 287-298
Conditional Residence (CR), 34-35
    Conditional Residence and the Citizenship Requirement, 35
    Getting rid of a Conditional Requirement, 35
    Investment, 34
    Marriage, 34
consular processing, 36

constitution, attachment to, 55
continuous physical presence requirement, 18, 51-52
continuous residence exception, 86
continuous residence requirement, 19-20, 49-50, 52
Deferred Action visa, 12-14
disability accommodations, 82-86
Diversity Lottery Visa, 31-33
English,
	exemptions, 80, 82
	learning, 10, 20-23, 93
	classes, 20-23
ESL (English as a Second Language), 20-21
exemptions, exceptions, modifications, 81-86
	civics, 81-82
	English, 80-81, 82
	medical disability, 82-86
	continuous residence exception, 86
fingerprints, 18, 59
flashcards, 9, 305-382
forms, citizenship and immigration
	AR-11 ("Change of Address"), 55-56
	cost, 42-43
	I-9, ("Form I-9, "Employment Eligibility Verification"), 27
	I-90 ("Application to Replace Permanent Resident card"), 42
	I-130 ("Petition for Alien Relative"), 30, 42
	I-131 ("Reentry Permit"), 40, 42
	I-140 ("Petition for Alien Worker"), 30, 42
	I-485 ("Application to Register PR Adjust Status"), 31
	I-526 ("Immigrant Petition by Alien Entrepreneur"), 30, 42
	I-551 ("Permanent Resident Card"), 34, 38
	I-864 ("Affadavit of Support"), 28, 42
	N-400 ("Application for Naturalization"), 84-85, 107-144
	N-426 ("Exemption for Military Personnel"), 51
	N-445 ("Notice of Naturalization Oath Ceremony"), 56
	N-470 ("Application to Preserve Residence"), 40, 42, 50
	N-565 ("Application for Replacement of Naturalization Document"), 43
	N-600 ("Application for Certificate of Citizenship"), 43
	N-648 ("Medical Certificate for Disability Exceptions"), 43, 82-86

green card, see *permanent resident visa*
immigration reform (2012), 12-14
interview advice, 107-111
interview question practice, 107-144
law/legal help, 37
letter, to USCIS with application, 63-64
literacy directory (website), 93
lottery number, visa, 31-33
medical disability certificate (N-648), 43, 82-85
military, exemptions, 51
moral character, 53-54
naturalization ceremony, 56-57
    form to reschedule, 56
Oath of Allegiance, 55-57, 102
    meaning, 103
Obama, Deferred Action visa, 12-14
Permanent resident visa ("green card"),
    adjustment of status, 35
    consular processing, 36
    description, 38
    family, immediate, 30
    filing for, 28-30
    how to get one, 28-32
    renewing when you're out of the country too long, 36-37
    rights, 6
    responsibilities, 6
    sponsors, 28, 30-31
Pledge of Allegiance, 101
photos, 18, 57, 59
reentry permit, 40-42
reading test, scoring, 71, 99
regional centers, addresses, 60-62
TOEFL (website), 93
translating, using Babelfish, 94
translating, using Google, 94
travel, record keeping, 109
undocumented immigrants, (see also *Obama*), 12-14
U.S. Immigration and Nationality Act, 29-30

verbs,
 past and present, 197
 regular, 198-201
 irregular, 202-207
 "be", 208-209
visas, changing status, 35-36
vocabulary,
 500 most common English words, 166-190
 USCIS vocabulary, reading, 148-151
 USCIS vocabulary, writing, 155-159
 USCIS vocabulary, reading/writing same lists, 161-162
 word pairs with opposite meanings, 191-194
 verbs, 197-209
websites, 89-94
 Bablefish translate, 94
 Google translate, 94
 government, U.S., 89-94
 Spanish (USCIS), 89
writing,
 interview answers to practice, 114-144
 sentences to practice, 214-221
 scoring of, 72, 99
 vocabulary, USCIS reading 148-151,
 vocabulary, USCIS writing 155-159
 vocabulary, USCIS words on both lists 166-190

CPSIA information can be obtained at www.ICGtesting.com
Printed in the USA
LVOW05s1749250913

354112LV00017B/808/P